TEACH it
Penance *and* Reconciliation

TEACH it

Penance *and* Reconciliation

Joseph D. White, Ph.D., & Ana Arista White

Our Sunday Visitor Publishing Division
Our Sunday Visitor, Inc.
Huntington, Indiana 46750

Nihil Obstat
Rev. Michael Heintz
Censor Librorum

Imprimatur
✠ John M. D'Arcy
Bishop of Fort Wayne-South Bend
December 12, 2003

The *nihil obstat* and *imprimatur* are official declarations that a book is free from doctrinal or moral error. It is not implied that those who have granted the *nihil obstat* and *imprimatur* agree with the contents, opinions, or statements expressed.

Our Sunday Visitor Publishing Division
Our Sunday Visitor, Inc.
200 Noll Plaza
Huntington, IN 46750

ISBN: 1-931709-88-2 (Inventory No. R43)

Cover design by Rebecca Heaston
Interior design by Sherri L. Hoffman
Illustrations by Mimi Sternhagen

PRINTED IN THE UNITED STATES OF AMERICA

Acknowledgements

Special thanks to Paz Rico for assistance with Spanish translations.
Thanks to Beth, Greg, Julianne, George, Jill, and all at Our Sunday Visitor for your support and skillful collaboration.

This book is dedicated to the catechists and families in the Faith Formation program
at St. Thomas Aquinas Catholic Church in College Station, Texas.
It has been a blessing to know and work with you.

Table of Contents

Introduction

What a privilege it is to share the sacraments with children and their families. The sacraments are treasures of our Catholic faith — vehicles of God's grace and opportunities to meet him in a personal way. The sacrament of reconciliation is our reminder that God loves us unconditionally and always welcomes us back to him. What an important and life-shaping message to pass on to our children!

IT BEGINS WITH GOD'S GREAT LOVE FOR US

God knows and loves each of us individually. He watches us closely and holds us in his care. Psalm 139:2-4 says, "Thou knowest when I sit down and when I rise up; thou discernest my thoughts from afar. Thou searchest out my path and my lying down, and art acquainted with all my ways. Even before a word is on my tongue, lo, O LORD, thou knowest it altogether." God created us out of his love and formed us in his own image. Understanding the sacrament of reconciliation begins most naturally in our awareness of God's great love and the dignity we share by virtue of our creation in his own likeness.

God showed his love most completely in the person of Jesus Christ, who called himself the Good Shepherd, welcomed children, reached out to the poor and marginalized, and gave his own life for the sins of the world. Christ is God's love personified, and it is Christ who meets us in the sacrament of reconciliation.

IT IS INEXTRICABLY TIED TO EDUCATION ABOUT OTHER SACRAMENTS, ESPECIALLY BAPTISM

A sacrament is a visible and concrete sign. God certainly could accomplish his work in other ways if he wished, but he chooses to work through the sacraments because he understands our need for concrete signs, so we can become more aware of his work and cooperate in a tangible way. In the sacrament of reconciliation, the priest represents both Christ and the Christian community. We are all part of the one, mystical Body of Christ, so our sin injures the whole Body. Simultaneous reconciliation with both Christ and the Church is crucial. In the act of absolution, we are offered a visible sign to reassure us that God and his Church really do forgive us and welcome us home. Could God forgive us of our sins without these signs if he wanted to? Of course he could, but he chooses to work in this way so we will have a visual aid to help us better understand the process.

Baptism is the sacrament whereby we are born into God's family, the Church, and receive God's gift of forgiveness. We "unwrap" that gift again and again in the sacrament of reconciliation. We can approach God in this intimate way by virtue of our adoption as his sons and daughters through baptism. For this reason, preparation for reconciliation (or any sacrament, for that matter) should include a deeper understanding of the gifts and the calling we received when we were baptized.

IT PRESENTS SIN HONESTLY

God made us, and he knows what we need to live a healthy and fulfilled life. We are failing to live up to all we could be when we stray from God's plan. Thus, speaking honestly about sin and our need to avoid it does not shame or degrade us; rather, it is an affirmation of our dignity as beings created in God's image. If we tell ourselves it's okay to sin sometimes because "nobody's perfect," we are selling ourselves short. We should strive to be the wonderful people he created us to be, and when we fail we should seek forgiveness and pray for the grace to do better.

IT PRECEDES CATECHESIS FOR FIRST RECEPTION OF THE EUCHARIST

True intimacy with Christ requires being able to approach him in humility, but without guilt or shame, with nothing to hide, and with full awareness of his love for us. Nothing in our Catholic faith more poignantly illustrates our intimacy with Christ (and with one another) than the Eucharist. But to really understand and experience that closeness, we must make sure we have taken care of anything that stands between ourselves and God. Therefore, the Church asks that first reception of the Eucharist be preceded by celebration of reconciliation.

Catechesis for reconciliation should be separate from catechesis for First Communion. They are two distinctly meaningful sacraments and should be experienced as such.

IT INVOLVES THE ENTIRE PARISH COMMUNITY, ESPECIALLY PARENTS

"Catechesis is a responsibility of the entire Christian community" (*General Directory for Catechesis*, 220). This is especially true of education about the sacraments, because they are our family celebrations of faith. Nevertheless, a child's own parents occupy a special role in the formation of their children for the sacraments. "Parents have the first responsibility for the education of their children," the *Catechism* states (2223). It's very important, then, for those of us who are catechists and directors of religious education to facilitate the passing on of the faith from parent to child through catechesis of parents and structured parent-child experiences. Tips for involving parents in parish-based sacramental catechesis are offered in the appendix of this book.

WHEN ARE CHILDREN READY TO CELEBRATE RECONCILIATION?

The truth of God's love for us is a source of such wonder and power that we want to share reconciliation with children as soon as they are ready. However, we want to make sure kids are prepared, developmentally, for the experience. So at what age are they ready to celebrate the sacrament? The answer depends somewhat on the individual child. Each child varies in the way he or she grows cognitively, emotionally, and spiritually. Still, there are some general trends that can give us insight into when kids are most likely to be ready.

In the preschool years, children are in what the Swiss psychologist Jean Piaget called the *preoperational* stage of cognitive development. They tend to see the world as being centered around them. Children this age sometimes attribute lifelike qualities to inanimate objects, and they tend to believe that things really are just as they appear. These children are still learning that most natural phenomena happen in certain, set ways. Preschool children sometimes tell elaborate stories that aren't true because they wish they were true. They haven't yet learned that what is real can't be changed by wishing it to be different. Kids this age are still getting a grasp on the difference between reality and fantasy, between truth and untruth. Morally, they often are more concerned about being caught doing something wrong than the "rightness" or "wrongness" of the action. Taking a cookie from the cookie jar may be okay if Mom's not looking, but not if she is. This is not so much a moral fault as a style of moral reasoning that reflects their developmental way of thinking.

Children in the *concrete operational* stage of development (which starts at about age six or seven) have moved past this sort of thinking and are aware that the world works according to certain rules. Concrete operational children have an elementary understanding of natural phenomena, and they understand that certain things are true and other things are not. They know that a mask and costume don't turn a person into someone else, and that there are logical explanations for magic tricks. (While preschool children may see magic tricks and say "wow," children in the concrete operational stage will ask, "How did you do that?") Just as they understand that there are rules for natural phenomena, children in the concrete operational stage understand that there are rules for behavior. Children this age are sometimes so preoccupied with "the rules" that they like to tattle on others who are not following them. They know there is a difference between right and wrong, and the "rightness" or "wrongness" of an action doesn't depend on who's watching.

In the Church, children at this stage of development are said to have reached the "age of reason." Knowledge of right and wrong has become more solidified and internalized, and children are better able to learn about a process of thinking that involves consulting their own consciences. It's no accident, then, that many children are prepared for reconciliation at about age seven. For most children, this is appropriate. Some caution is needed, however; not every child reaches the age of reason at the same time. For some it comes earlier, and for some it may come later. Pay individual attention to each child's understanding of right and wrong to ensure that each is properly disposed to celebrate the sacrament.

HOW TO USE THIS BOOK

This book is intended to be a resource for the catechist or DRE preparing children for first reconciliation. It is divided according to several major topics in reconciliation catechesis. Each topic begins with "Know It" pages for the catechist. These pages summarize Catholic teaching about the topic and offer an overview of how children's cognitive, emotional, social, and moral development affect learning and understanding of the topic. Next come "Teach It" pages, which provide practical suggestions for conveying the information on this topic to the children with whom you are working. These pages include hands-on activities, such as games, arts and crafts projects, and object lessons, as well as tips on discussing abstract concepts in a way children will understand. Finally, we have included "Share It" pages, which summarize basic content for parents and offer suggestions for sharing the lessons at home.

May God bless you as you share his eternal and unfailing love with his children!

God's Great Love

God's Great Love

Each one of us, in our very essence, is an expression of God's love. God created us in love, and out of love he reveals himself to us. "God is love, " Scripture tells us (1 John 4:8). So unless we have some understanding of the love of God, we've not only missed an *important* point, we've missed the *whole* point! God knows each of us by name, and watches us closely. Psalm 139 speaks of a God who knows our words before we say them, who discerns our very thoughts from a distance. God watches us so closely because he cares about us and *wants* to know us.

God shows his love for us in many ways. First, **he created us in his own image** (see Genesis 1:26). Of all the creatures on the earth, human beings are most like God. As beings created in God's image, we are, by nature, good. (Excellent, in fact!)

God shows his love through the rest of creation. He has given us everything we need, and he tells us not to worry about what we will eat or wear, but to work together to bring about his plan of caring for all of his creation, especially our fellow human beings.

God shows his love to us through the guidelines he gives us for living. Because he created us, he knows what's best for us — what will truly lead us to fulfillment. He has communicated these guidelines to us through Scripture and Church teaching.

God shows his love through loving people in our lives. Family members and friends who care for us according to God's plan were given to us as models of the Father's love.

Finally, **God shows his love most completely in the person of Jesus Christ.** Jesus reached out in love to those who were most despised by the world — people guilty of public sin, the diseased, the poorest of the poor, and the otherwise marginalized. Many times in Scripture we read about Jesus becoming almost overwhelmed with compassion for people. He ministered to them sometimes to the point of exhaustion because he loved them so much.

Jesus told stories about God's love as well. He told of a shepherd who loved each of his sheep so much that he was willing to search for one that was lost and lead it to safety (Matthew 18:12-14). He taught about a father whose son renounced his family and squandered his inheritance, only to realize the error of his ways and return to ask if he could be one of the servants in his former home. When the father saw his son coming home, he ran to meet him, threw his arms around him, and had a great feast to celebrate (see Luke 15:11-32). The message is clear: Nothing — *nothing* — can separate us from God's love. "For I am sure that neither death, nor life, nor angels, nor principalities, nor things present, nor things to come, nor powers, nor height, nor depth, nor anything else in all creation, will be able to separate us from the love of God in Christ Jesus our Lord" (Romans 8:38-39).

HOW CHILDREN UNDERSTAND GOD'S LOVE

Children first learn about love from their primary caretakers, most typically their parents. When they are very young, they are completely dependent on adults. When adults respond to them with love and care, they learn that they can trust others to meet their needs. As children grow older, they hopefully learn that they are loved even when they displease their parents, but this unconditional love becomes a motivator for doing better. Children who truly love their parents want to please them. They want Mom or Dad to be proud. The natural relationship between parents and children illustrates how the family is designed by God as a school of holiness. We learn about God and how to relate to him from our relationship to our loved ones (and vice versa). Often our first glimpse of the love of God is the love we are shown by our parents. In any family, these relationships are only an imperfect image of what God is like. But a family that is working at following God's plan will at least offer a taste of the relationship God wants to have with us.

The parish is another place children can learn about God's love. They hear stories about God in religious education classes and Mass, but more importantly, they learn about God's love by experiencing the Christian community. As catechists of children, we must always be aware that we are representing Christ in a profound way to the children to whom we minister. They should experience the parish (and especially the parts of parish life designed especially for them) as welcoming places in which they are valued as individuals. This is all the more important given the prevalence of family stress and discord in modern society. The parish should be one place where each child *knows* he or she is loved.

Because of their concrete style of thinking, children will only be able to have a clear concept of a God who loves them if they can "put a face on God." They must have loving relationships with others to understand the love God has for them.

In addition to the recommendations offered in the "Teach It" pages for teaching children about God's love, we must be conscious of how our interactions with children can be teaching tools. Greeting each child by name, allowing them to share their stories and prayer requests, and respecting their individual contributions to the group can be powerful illustrations of the love of God. When we are conscious of the message we wish to send, we can help personify the love God has for each of these little ones.

God's Great Love

God's Gifts of Love

MAIN POINT

We can learn about God's love for us by paying attention to the wonderful gifts he gives.

MATERIALS NEEDED

- ❑ red poster board, cut into quarter sheets (one quarter sheet for each student)
- ❑ white ribbon
- ❑ hole punch
- ❑ magazines with pictures of families, food, and nature
- ❑ glue (enough for the children to share)
- ❑ holy cards with the infant Jesus
- ❑ scissors (one pair for each child)

PREPARATION

Cut a heart shape out of each quarter sheet of red poster board. Using the hole punch, make two holes in the tops of the hearts.

INSTRUCTIONS

Tell the children that when we realize the blessings God has given us, we know that he loves and cares for us. Give each child a poster board heart. Ask the children to cut pictures out of the magazines that remind us of the blessings God has given us (families, food, animals, or trees, for example) and glue the pictures to the hearts. Give each child a holy card and mention that God's greatest gift to us was his Son, Jesus. Have the kids glue the holy card in the middle of the heart. Finally, assist the children in tying the ribbon through the holes in the top of the heart into a bow, as one would tie on the top of a present.

Find the Lost Sheep

MAIN POINT

God knows each of us by name, and he looks for us when we have strayed away from him.

MATERIALS NEEDED

- ❑ Reproducible: "Sheep Pictures"
- ❑ scissors
- ❑ masking tape
- ❑ statue of Jesus, the Good Shepherd

PREPARATION

Make enough copies of "Sheep Pictures" so there is a sheep picture for each child. Cut out the sheep pictures, and put one child's name on each of the sheep. Hide the pictures around the classroom. (Think creatively — children are not always easy to fool. Try taping the sheep to the bottom of the chairs, underneath the chalk tray, in inconspicuous places on the wall, etc.) Create a Good Shepherd altar in a visible space in the room. Place a cloth underneath it (you may wish to use the current liturgical color).

INSTRUCTIONS

Tell the parable of the lost sheep. Explain that Jesus told this story to help us understand that God knows each of us by name and feels sad when we aren't following him. When we aren't doing what God wants us to do, we are like a lost sheep. God wants us to be safe and happy, and he will look for us. He is happy when we come back to him. Tell the children that there are several "lost sheep" around the room. Explain that each child has his or her own sheep. Ask the children to find their "lost sheep" and bring it back to the Good Shepherd. They can place their sheep around the Good Shepherd statue. If they find a sheep with someone else's name, they should leave that one and look for their own. However, if they have already found their own sheep and there are children who would like help finding theirs, they may help others. After all the sheep have been found, explain to the children that the sacrament of reconciliation, which they are preparing to celebrate this year, is God's way of bringing us back to him when we are lost. Remind them that God always welcomes us back, and he is happy when we come to him.

Sheep Pictures

Rejoice with me because I have found my lost sheep!

God's Beautiful World

MAIN POINT

God's love for us is evident in the beauty of creation.

MATERIALS NEEDED

- ❑ light blue butcher paper
- ❑ construction paper in various colors (including brown, green, and yellow)
- ❑ several pairs of scissors
- ❑ found nature objects (such as grasses, leaves, small pebbles)
- ❑ glue (one bottle for each child)

PREPARATION

Cut a five-foot-long piece of butcher paper and lay it across a table in the classroom or on the floor. Arrange to take the kids on a short walk at the beginning of the session.

INSTRUCTIONS

Take the children on a short nature hike. Encourage them to find grasses, leaves, small pebbles, and other objects they can use to create a class mural to illustrate the beauty of nature. Tell them that when we consider how beautiful the world is and see the care God took in creating it, we know that he loves and cares for us as well. When you return to the classroom, encourage the children to make a mural showing the beauty of the natural world. They may want to combine construction paper and their found objects (for example, they might make a tree trunk out of construction paper, then glue leaves to the top of the trunk). The finished product can be hung on a wall in the class-room.

Dear Parents,

Our session today focused on God's great love for us. God knows each one of us, and nothing can separate us from his love. He shows his love in many ways, including:

- our creation in his own image,
- the rest of creation, which includes everything we need,
- the guidelines he gives us for living so we can be truly happy,
- family and friends who love and care for us, and
- his son, Jesus, who taught about God's love through his actions and words, and who gave his own life as a sacrifice for us.

Please review these main points with your child. One way you can do this is to have a prayer time (perhaps before a family meal) in which each family member names a blessing God has given your family. Another way to explore God's love is to go for a walk outside and talk about the beauty of creation, noting that God provides for all of his creatures. Above all, remember that God uses you as a parent to show his love to your child. Be sure to remind your child that you love him or her, and always will.

God bless,

COMPÁRTALO

El Gran Amor de Dios

Estimados padres de familia,

Nuestra sesión de hoy se enfocó en el gran amor de Dios para con nosotros. Dios nos conoce a cada uno de nosotros, y nada nos puede separar de su amor. Él nos muestra su amor de muchas maneras, incluyendo:

- nuestra creación a su misma imagen,
- el resto de la creación, que incluye todo lo que necesitamos,
- las normas que él nos da para vivir para que podamos ser verdaderamente felices,
- familia y amigos que nos aman y que se preocupan por nosotros, y
- su hijo, Jesús, que enseñó sobre el amor de Dios a través de sus acciones y de sus palabras, y que dio su propia vida como sacrificio para nosotros.

Por favor revisen estos puntos principales con su hijo o hija. Una manera que usted puede hacer esto es tener una hora para rezar (tal vez antes de la comida) en que cada miembro de la familia nombra una bendición que Dios le ha mandado a su familia. Otra manera de explorar el amor de Dios es salir a caminar afuera y hablar sobre la belleza de la creación, mencionando que Dios provee para todas sus criaturas. Por encima de todo, recuerde que Dios lo usa a usted como padre o madre para demostrar su amor hacia su hijo o hija. Asegúrese de recordarle a su hijo o hija que usted lo o la ama, y que siempre lo o la amará.

Que Dios los Bendiga,

God's Rules for Living

God's Rules for Living

Another key point of Jesus' moral teaching is that *morality is rooted in love*. When asked about the greatest commandment, Jesus replied: "You shall love the Lord your God with all your heart, and with all your soul, and with all your mind. This is the great and first commandment. And a second is like it: You shall love your neighbor as yourself. On these two commandments depend all the law and the prophets" (Matthew 22:37-39).

THE TEN COMMANDMENTS

The Ten Commandments (Exodus 20:1-17) serve as a guide for the rules of godly living. To more accurately grasp the meaning of the Ten Commandments, it is useful to look at them within the context of the two Christian principles listed above. As Jesus said, all the commandments relate to love of God and love of others. The first three commandments speak of loving God. "You shall have no other gods before me" refers not only to worship of other gods, but is an admonition to put God above all other things in our lives. The second commandment, "You shall not take the name of the Lord your God in vain," reminds us to keep God's name holy. This commandment is not just about using God's name as profanity. It reminds us to treat God's name with honor and respect and avoid bringing disrepute to God's name by taking false oaths or uttering blasphemy. The third commandment, to keep the Sabbath day holy, is truly a gift from God. Under the Old Covenant, the Jewish people observed Saturday as a day to rest and give thanks to God for his goodness. The *Catechism* states, "The sabbath, which represented the completion of the first creation, has been replaced by Sunday which recalls the new creation inaugurated by the Resurrection of Christ" (2190). We can easily get caught up in a hectic pace and forget what life is all about. For this reason, we are *commanded* by God to take a break and appreciate him and his creation. In Canon Law and the *Catechism*, Sunday is called the "foremost holy day of obligation." We gather on Sunday to give thanks to God in the Eucharist.

The fourth through tenth commandments relate to loving others. The fourth commandment calls us to honor our parents, but also affects our relationships with others. We are to honor each person as an individual with inherent dignity, created in God's image. Concerning the fifth commandment, Jesus said, "You have heard that it was said to the men of old, 'You shall not kill; and whoever kills shall be liable to judgment.' But I say to you that every one who is angry with his brother shall be liable to judgment" (Matthew 5:21-22). Again, challenging us to go past behavior itself to the attitudes of the heart, Jesus points out that we cannot be the people God created us to be while we create barriers between ourselves and others by feeding our anger or refusing to forgive. The commandments themselves call us to an examination of the heart when we are told not only to avoid adultery (sixth commandment), but also to avoid lust (tenth commandment). The root of sinful sexual behavior is the objectification of the body, looking at ourselves or others as "things" to be used, rather than beings created by God. The seventh and ninth commandments call us to avoid theft (seventh commandment), but again go further to address the attitude that would give rise to theft (ninth commandment). We should be happy with what we have, knowing that God has blessed each of us in many ways. Finally, the eighth commandment, "You shall not bear false witness against your neighbor" (Exodus 20:16), calls us to live in and bear witness to the truth and to build one another up rather than injuring the reputation of others.

VIRTUE AND THE WORK OF THE HOLY SPIRIT

Both the charity to which we are called and the inheritance we are offered are outlined by Christ in the Beatitudes. Under the old covenant, God promised to bless Abraham and his descendants and to make their name great (see Genesis 12:3). Under the new covenant, Christ echoes these promises by announcing the blessing of those who live lives of charity and humility (*Catechism of the Catholic Church*, 1716-1717). To them he promises the kingdom of heaven, inheritance of the earth, and the title "sons of God" (Matthew 5:3-9).

We grow in our ability to live a moral life as we accept the truth about ourselves as beings created in God's image. We are created to be like God, which is the goal of a virtuous life (se *Catechism of the Catholic Church,* 1803). Through the Holy Spirit's work within us and the grace God gives us in the sacraments, we grow in our love for God and others and, consequently, in virtuous behavior. It is a formation of heart, rooted in love, directed by God.

HOW CHILDREN UNDERSTAND GOD'S RULES

As mentioned in the introduction to this book, children between ages seven and eleven are in what psychologists call the "concrete operational" stage of thinking. They think in very concrete, rules-based, black-and-white terms. Because most environments for children include rules for their behavior, and because children are fairly attentive to rules at this age, the idea that God would have rules for them comes naturally. The real challenges in working with young children on this topic are in communicating God's rules in a form they can understand and teaching them how to apply these guidelines to their everyday lives. It's helpful to begin with some reasoning about *why* God's rules would be important and valid for us. Because God made us, he knows what's best for us. Children this age have usually experienced a time when ignoring their parent's rules led to negative consequences they didn't foresee, so this concept makes sense to them. The following pages include some tips for helping children understand how God's rules apply to them and their unique situations.

God's Rules for Living

Ten Commandments Tick-Tack-Toe

MAIN POINT

We can apply God's rules, the Ten Commandments, to our everyday lives in a variety of situations.

MATERIALS NEEDED

- ❑ chalkboard and chalk or flip chart and marker
- ❑ Reproducible: "Situation Cards"
- ❑ Reproducible: "The Ten Commandments" (one copy for each child)

PREPARATION

Draw a large tick-tack-toe grid on the chalkboard or flip chart. Make one copy of "Situation Cards." Cut out the cards and place them in an envelope.

INSTRUCTIONS

Give each child a copy of The Ten Commandments. Divide the class into two teams, with half of the group being the X's and half the O's. Decide which team will go first, then take a Situation Card out of the envelope. Present the situation, then ask the team to respond as a group to two questions: 1) What choice should you make? 2) Which one of the Ten Commandments would help you know what to do? Give the team a few seconds to agree on their answer and have them choose a spokesperson. If the team answers correctly, they get to put an X or an O on the board. If they answer incorrectly, the question falls to the other team. Keep alternating between teams until one team wins or the grid is full.

1. A friend invites you to play at a time when you have religious education class at church. Your teacher said it would be an important lesson.

2. You are going to the movies with a friend. She wants to see a movie that you know your parents do not want you to watch.

3. Some kids at school are using God's name to say bad words.

4. You found a really cool toy on the playground at school.

5. One of your friends is making funny faces at you during Mass.

6. Some of the girls at school are saying mean things about a new girl. You think the things they are saying aren't even true.

7. Your mother tells you to clean your room. You feel like playing video games instead.

8. Some kids at school are telling bad jokes.

9. You are angry at your brother and feel like hitting him.

10. You like your friend's new bike and all you can think about is how to get one like it.

Answer Key

Situation 1	First Commandment
Situation 2	Fourth or Ninth Commandments
Situation 3	Second Commandment
Situation 4	Seventh Commandment
Situation 5	Third Commandment
Situation 6	Eighth Commandment
Situation 7	Fourth Commandment
Situation 8	Ninth or Sixth Commandment
Situation 9	Fifth Commandment
Situation 10	Tenth or Seventh Commandment

The Ten Commandments

1. Make God the most important thing in your life.

2. Use God's name the proper way.

3. Make Sunday a day to worship God.

4. Love your parents and follow their rules.

5. Be kind to the people and animals God made.

6. Be respectful in the things you do with your body.

7. Take care of other people's things; don't take what belongs to someone else.

8. Tell the truth.

9. Keep your thoughts and words clean.

10. Be happy with the things you have.

Duck, Duck, Disciple!

MAIN POINT

A disciple is someone who follows Jesus by doing what Jesus would do.

MATERIALS NEEDED

Area large enough for the children to sit in a circle with some room around the outside of the circle.

PREPARATION

None

INSTRUCTIONS

This is a takeoff of the old, familiar "Duck, Duck, Goose" game. Have the students sit in a circle with about one foot of space between each child. Choose one child to be "it." That child will walk around the outside of the circle, tapping each child lightly on the shoulder and saying "Duck, Duck, Duck" until he or she finally gets to the child he or she wants to name "Disciple!" The child who's chosen to be the "disciple" chases "it" around the circle. If "it" makes it back to the disciple's space first, he or she sits down and names one way to follow (or be like) Jesus (obeying parents or being kind to others, for example).

The Two Greatest Commandments

MAIN POINT

Jesus taught that all of God's law is summed up in two commandments: to "love the Lord your God with all your heart, and with all your soul, and with all your mind" and to "love your neighbor as yourself" (Matthew 22:37-39). If we really follow this Law of Love, we will do what God asks of us.

MATERIALS NEEDED

- ❑ Bible
- ❑ Reproducibles: "The Two Greatest Commandments" and "Commandments to Cut and Paste" (one copy for each child)
- ❑ scissors (one pair for each child)
- ❑ glue

PREPARATION

Mark Matthew 22:35-40 in your Bible.

INSTRUCTIONS

Read Matthew 22:35-40 to the children. Explain that Jesus was saying if we really love God with all our heart and love others as well as ourselves, we will be following all God's rules for our lives. Give each child a copy of "Commandments to Cut and Paste." Ask each to cut out the commandments and glue them on the tablets on "The Two Greatest Commandments" to show which commandments are about loving God and which commandments are about loving others and self. (Note: While all the commandments could technically apply to loving God, some are more specifically focused on our behavior toward ourselves and others. The first three commandments apply to loving God above all things. Commandments four though ten are about how we treat others and ourselves.)

The Two Greatest Commandments!

Love self and others

Love God

Make God the most important thing in your life.

Use God's name the proper way.

Make Sunday a day to worship God.

Love your parents and follow their rules.

Be kind to the people and animals God made.

Be respectful in the things you do with your body.

Take care of other people's things; don't take what belongs to someone else.

Tell the truth.

Keep your thoughts and words clean.

Be happy with the things you have.

SHARE IT

God's Rules for Living

Dear Parents,

God created us in his image to be holy and happy people. He knows what is best for us and gives us guidelines for living. Today in class we talked about God's rules, the Ten Commandments, which are found in Scripture in Exodus Chapter 20.

When Jesus was asked which commandment was the greatest, he said "You shall love the Lord your God with all your heart, and with all your soul, and with all your mind. This is the great and first commandment. And a second is like it: You shall love your neighbor as yourself. On these two commandments depend all the law and the prophets" (Matthew 22:37-40). All of God's rules for us are about loving God, others, and self.

Elementary school children are very conscious of rules, and they have rules to follow in almost every environment. The concrete, rule-based thinking of children this age makes this a great time to talk about God's rules. This week at home, talk about your family's rules and how they relate to God's rules for living. It may be especially helpful to highlight the "Law of Love" Jesus gave us as the "greatest commandments" and how your family's rules relate to this important teaching.

God Bless,

Estimados padres de familia,

Dios nos creó a su imagen para ser personas santas y felices. Él sabe qué es lo mejor para nosotros y nos da normas para vivir. Hoy en la clase hablamos sobre las reglas de Dios, los Diez Mandamientos, que se encuentran en la Sagrada Escritura en el libro de Éxodos Capítulo 20.

Cuando le preguntaron a Jesús, cuál era el mandamiento más importante, él dijo "Amarás al Señor tu Dios con todo tu corazón, y con toda tu alma, y con toda tu mente. Este es el gran y primer mandamiento. El segundo es igual: Amarás a tu vecino como a ti mismo. De estos dos mandamientos dependen toda la ley y los profetas" (Mateo 22:37-40). Todas las reglas de Dios para nosotros son de amar a Dios, a los demás, y a uno mismo.

Los niños y las niñas de la primaria están muy conscientes de las reglas, y ellos tienen reglas a seguir en casi todo medio ambiente. La manera de pensar de los niños a esta edad es concreta, en base a las reglas y esto hace que sea un gran momento para hablarles sobre las reglas de Dios. Esta semana en su casa, hable sobre las reglas de su familia y cómo se relacionan con las reglas de Dios para vivir. Será una gran ayuda destacar la "Ley del Amor" que Jesús nos dio como los "más importantes mandamientos" y cómo se relacionan las reglas de su familia a esta enseñanza importante.

Que Dios los Bendiga,

Sin and Conscience

Sin and Conscience

God created us in his image to love and serve him. When God created human beings, he had a beautiful plan for each of us to live according to his will and, in doing so, to be truly blessed. Because he loves us and wants us to *choose* right over wrong, God gave human beings free will, the ability to determine our actions. The first humans, Adam and Eve, wanted the power God had, and in their selfishness, they let pride take over. Their pride brought sin and death into the world, and sin became intertwined with human nature. This flaw, called "original sin," was passed on throughout history. God created us in his image to do good things, but the flaw of original sin leads us to act against our true nature. Although people are good by nature, original sin keeps us from acting that way.

SIN: MISSING THE MARK

The word "sin" literally means "missing the mark." We sin when we choose to miss the great things God has intended for us. This is an important point. No one knows better than the Creator how to care for that which is created. When we buy a complex piece of machinery, we attend to the manufacturer's instructions for caring for the machine. In a similar way, God provides instruction out of love and care for us, knowing that we bring damaging consequences upon ourselves when we behave outside his will. The most damaging consequence of our sin is the fact that through sin we separate ourselves from God, who is the source of all good things.

Individuals are guilty of mortal sin if they intentionally and with full knowledge violate God's law in a serious (or "grave") matter. Grave matters include murder, adultery, theft, bearing false witness, defrauding another, or dishonoring one's parents. Those sins are not necessarily mortal sins, but they are serious enough to be mortal sins if they are committed with full intention and knowledge. Venial sin is any violation of God's law that does not meet the criteria for mortal sin. Venial sin weakens the work of God in our lives. It harms us because it keeps us from being the people God made us to be. God forgives our venial sins, but they do damage to our own souls and to others.

FORMING A CONSCIENCE

God has given each of us a conscience, which helps us decide the "rightness" or "wrongness" of actions. But our consciences must be correctly formed through learning about God's will for our lives. We form our consciences through study of Scripture and Church teaching, as well as prayer and openness to God's grace and guidance. In an "examination of conscience," we think about our actions in light of God's will, comparing the things we have done (and haven't done) with God's guidelines for our lives.

HOW CHILDREN UNDERSTAND SIN AND CONSCIENCE

Concrete thinkers, young children can understand actions as right or wrong; but they sometimes have difficulty understanding motives. This can lead to some confusion over exactly what is a sin and what isn't. Children who forget to do something they were asked to do may think they have disobeyed, for example.

It's important that kids understand the difference between a *sin* and an *accident* or *mistake*. Catechists can help make this distinction clear by posing hypothetical situations and asking the children to tell whether what is described would be a sin or an accident. To help make this distinction clear, we as adults should avoid getting overly upset or punitive for rule infractions that are truly accidental. But we also should point out that feeling sorry about a wrong choice does not make that choice an accident. The real question is, "Did we do it on purpose?"

Young children have only a vague concept of what a conscience is. We can help them get in touch with this concept by asking if they have ever, when faced with a choice, heard a little voice inside their heads say, "Don't do that, it's wrong," or "Do this, it's the right thing to do." Most of them have experienced this phenomenon, even if they didn't know it was their conscience at work. Explain that this "little silent voice that is more like a thought" is from God, and depends on learning about God to tell us the right things to do. Learning about God's rules is the way we train this voice to tell us what choices to make.

Sin and Conscience

Sin or Accident?

MAIN POINT

A sin is a wrong choice. An accident is something we didn't choose to do. Feeling sorry for a wrong choice doesn't make it an accident. The real question is, "Did we do it on purpose?"

MATERIALS NEEDED

- ❑ Reproducible: "Is It a Sin or an Accident?"
- ❑ pencil or pen for each child

PREPARATION

Make a copy of "Is It a Sin or an Accident?" for each child.

INSTRUCTIONS

Briefly discuss the main points of this activity with the children. Be sure to note that when we make a wrong choice without really thinking it through, such an action is not really an accident, because we have a responsibility to think about our choices in light of God's rules. Some things go wrong, however, that we really didn't mean to do. An accident is not a sin. We can learn from accidents and be more careful the next time.

Give each child pen or pencil and a copy of "Is It a Sin or an Accident?" Read each scenario aloud and ask the children to circle "Sin" if they think the child sinned or "Accident" if they think the child's actions were an accident. After giving the children an opportunity to circle their answer, discuss the answer as a group. (This gives children who answered incorrectly the opportunity to receive corrective feedback in a non-threatening way.)

Is It a Sin or an Accident?

Sin You tripped while at your grandmother's house and broke her favorite vase. **Accident!**

Sin The kids at school were making fun of another kid. You joined in because you thought that you would look cool. **Accident!**

Sin Your sneaky sister jumped out in front of you. You were startled and bonked her in the head. **Accident!**

Sin You tripped while at your grandmother's house, broke her favorite vase, and blamed the broken vase on your cousin. **Accident!**

Sin You decided to daydream in Mass instead of paying attention. **Accident!**

A Child-Friendly Examination of Conscience

MAIN POINT

Examining our conscience means thinking about what we have done in light of God's rules.

MATERIALS NEEDED

❏ Reproducible: "Examination of Conscience"

PREPARATION

Make a copy of "Examination of Conscience" for each child.

INSTRUCTIONS

Some catechists prefer to wait until First Reconciliation day to ask the children to make a formal examination of conscience. Doing this a few weeks in advance, however, can help children begin to look through the lens of God's vision for us and identify areas in which they are struggling. This can make their experience of First Reconciliation much more meaningful.

If you use this activity before First Reconciliation, explain to the children that you will be looking at some questions to help them decide how well they are following God's rules. Explain that everyone has problems sometimes with God's rules, so they shouldn't feel bad about themselves if they identify some sins in their lives, but because God made us to do good things and knows what's best for us, we should always try hard to follow the guidelines he has given us. God will help us follow his rules more closely if we ask him to, and he always loves and forgives us when we are ready to accept his mercy.

Examination of Conscience

☆ Have I put God first, or have I sometimes made other things in my life more important than God? Do I remember to talk to him? Do I choose what God wants for me over what I want for myself?

☆ Have I used God's name with care, or have I used God's name in the wrong way (saying "God" when I wasn't really talking about him)?

☆ Have I tried hard to worship God at Mass by singing, praying, and listening, or have I misbehaved during Mass?

☆ Have I obeyed my parents — even when they are not looking? Have I talked back to them?

☆ Have I been kind to others? Have I solved disagreements in a peaceful way, or have I fought with anyone?

☆ Have I followed God's rules in how I treat my body and respect the bodies of others?

☆ Have I respected other peoples' things, or have I taken something that does not belong to me?

☆ Have I told the truth, or have I told a lie or said things that were only partly true?

☆ Have I kept my thoughts and words clean? Have I told or listened to bad jokes? Have I watched any movies or shows that I shouldn't have seen? Have I tried to keep my mind on good things?

☆ Have I been happy with the things I have, or have I been jealous of others?

Looking at Choices

MAIN POINT

Thinking about our choices in light of God's rules can help us see the ways in which we need to grow. We can identify hurts that need to be healed and struggles we can bring to God in the sacrament of reconciliation.

MATERIALS NEEDED

- ❏ Reproducible: "Choices"
- ❏ Reproducible: "The Ten Commandments"
- ❏ Pens or pencils for each child

PREPARATION

Make copies of "The Ten Commandments" and "Choices" for each child.

INSTRUCTIONS

Explain to the children that you will be reading short stories about kids their age and the choices they have made. Ask them to pay special attention to whether the children in the stories are following God's rules, the Ten Commandments. After each of the stories, have the children discuss their answers to the questions printed on their worksheet.

STORY 1

On Saturday afternoon, Darius's mother told him he needed to pick up his room before he did anything else. Darius started working on it, but when he was only about halfway through, Darius' friend Daniel came over and asked if he could play. Darius really wanted to go, so he told himself he would finish cleaning his room later. He shoved the rest of the mess under his bed to hide it and went outside to play.

Darius and Daniel had some trouble getting along that day. Darius wanted to play soccer, but Daniel wanted to ride bikes. "We always have to do what *you* want to do," complained Daniel. "I'm going to ride my bike. If you don't want to ride with me, that's fine." Daniel began to pedal away on his bike. Darius was so angry, he kicked the soccer ball at Daniel's bike. This caused Daniel to swerve and fall to the ground. Darius had hurt his friend. He went home feeling sad, thinking about the choices he had made that day. When Darius got home, his mother was in his room. He could tell she had seen what was under his bed.

STORY 2

Marisa got all the gifts she wanted at her birthday party Saturday night. The next morning, she was playing with her new toys when her dad told her it was time to get ready for Mass. Marisa didn't listen to her dad the first two times she was told. She wanted to keep playing with her toys instead. Marisa finally followed her dad's directions after he said he might have to put her new things away for a few days.

At Mass, Marisa played with the hymnal instead of singing. While the priest was reading the Gospel, she was making faces at a friend nearby.

STORY 3

Katie spent the night at a friend's house. Her friend had a CD that Katie was not allowed to buy because of the bad language in some of the songs. Katie listened to the CD with her friend, and they sang along with the songs. One of the songs even used God's name in a disrespectful way. They sang along with that one, too. When it was time for Katie to go home, she snuck the CD into her bag while her friend wasn't looking. "She'll just think she lost it, and she'll get another one at the mall, but my parents won't let me get it," Katie said to herself. When Katie got home, she began to wonder about some of the choices she had made.

STORY 4

Matthew had a spelling test at school. He hadn't studied and didn't know some of the words. Sophie was sitting nearby, and she always knew the right answers. Matthew copied the words he didn't know off her paper. Matthew's teacher, Ms. Chen, thought she saw Matthew copying, and she walked over to his desk. "Matthew, are you keeping your eyes on your paper?" his teacher asked. "Yes, Ms. Chen," answered Matthew.

Later that day, Matthew noticed that his best friend had a cool new backpack. Matthew liked it so much he couldn't stop thinking about it. He kept thinking about how to get one just like it. When Matthew got home and asked his mom about it, she said, "Matthew, you already have a nice backpack. We can't spend that much money on something you don't really need." "You never get me anything I want!" said Matthew, and he stormed off to his room. When he had calmed down, he felt sorry about how he had acted. He also began to think about other choices he had made that day.

Choices

Think about the choices Darius made. Did he break some of God's rules?
Which ones?
What should he do to make things right?

Think about Marisa's choices.
Did she choose to follow God's rules?
What should Marisa do now?

Why is Katie beginning to get a "funny feeling" about her choices?
Which of God's rules did she break?
How can she make things right?

Why is Matthew feeling sorry?
Whom has he hurt with his actions?
Did Matthew break some of God's rules? Which ones?
What should he do now?

The Ten Commandments

❶ Make God the most important thing in your life.

❷ Use God's name the proper way.

❸ Make Sunday a day to worship God.

❹ Love your parents and follow their rules.

❺ Be kind to the people and animals God made.

❻ Be respectful in the things you do with your body.

❼ Take care of other people's things; don't take what belongs to someone else.

❽ Tell the truth.

❾ Keep your thoughts and words clean.

❿ Be happy with the things you have.

Dear Parents,

In class we learned about the concepts of sin and examination of conscience. As concrete thinkers, young children can understand that actions are right or wrong, but they sometimes have difficulty understanding motives. They can be confused about exactly what is a sin and what isn't. Children who forget to do something they were asked to do may think they have disobeyed, for example.

To form their consciences appropriately, children need to understand the difference between a *sin* and an *accident* or *mistake*. Parents can help make this distinction by pointing out examples in their own family's lives, such as when something is accidentally dropped and broken, or when a child intentionally disobeys. Avoid becoming overly upset or punitive about truly accidental infractions at home, but point out that feeling sorry about a wrong choice we have made does not make that choice an accident. The real question is, "Did we do it on purpose?"

Young children have only a vague concept of what a conscience is. We can help them get in touch with this concept by asking if they have ever, when faced with a choice, heard a little voice inside their heads say, "Don't do that, it's wrong," or "Do this, it's the right thing to do." Most of them have experienced this phenomenon, even if they didn't know that it was their conscience at work. Explain that this "little silent voice that is more like a thought" is from God, and depends on learning about God to tell us the right things to do. Learning about God's rules is the way we train this voice to tell us what choices to make. When we have formed our consciences appropriately, we can look at our actions in light of what God wants and know when we have done the right thing or when we need to be reconciled with God and with others.

God Bless,

COMPÁRTALO

El Pecado y la Conciencia

Estimados padres de familia,

En la clase aprendimos sobre el concepto del pecado y el examen de conciencia.

Como pensadores concretos, los niños pequeños pueden entender que las acciones son buenas o malas, pero tienen a veces dificultad entendiendo los motivos. Ellos pueden estar confundidos sobre exactamente qué es un pecado y qué no es un pecado. Por ejemplo, a los niños que se les olvida hacer algo que se les pidió que hicieran pueden pensar que han desobedecido.

Para formarles apropiadamente la conciencia, los niños necesitan entender la diferencia entre un *pecado* y un *accidente* o un *error*. Los papás pueden ayudar a aclarar esto usando ejemplos en las vidas de sus propias familias, tal como cuando algo se cae accidentalmente y se quiebra, o cuando un niño desobedece intencionalmente. Evite enojarse demasiado o castigar demasiado sobre infracciones verdaderamente accidentales en la casa, pero señale que sentirse arrepentido por una mala selección que hayamos hecho no quiere decir que esa selección sea un accidente. La verdadera pregunta es "¿Lo hicimos a propósito?"

Los niños pequeños tienen únicamente un vago concepto sobre lo que es una conciencia. Nosotros les podemos ayudar a entender este concepto al preguntarles si alguna vez, cuando tuvieron que tomar una decisión, escucharon una pequeña voz dentro de ellos que decía "Es malo, no hagas eso," o "Has esto, es correcto lo que vas a hacer." La mayoría de ellos han sentido este fenómeno, aunque no sabían que era el trabajo de su conciencia. Explique que esta "pequeña voz silenciosa que es más como un pensamiento" viene de Dios y depende de aprender sobre Dios para que nos diga cuáles son las cosas que debemos hacer. Aprendiendo sobre las reglas de Dios es la manera en que entrenamos a esta voz para que nos diga lo que debemos hacer. Cuando hayamos formado nuestras conciencias apropiadamente, podremos ver cuando nuestras acciones son lo que Dios quiere y saber cuando hemos hecho lo correcto o cuándo necesitamos reconciliarnos con Dios y con otros.

Que Dios los Bendiga,

Baptism and Other Sacraments

Baptism and Other Sacraments

Jesus spent a great deal of time focusing on the truth that the visible, physical world is temporary. The physical world is only a sign of the invisible, spiritual realm — the realm of God the Father. Our physical bodies will pass away, but they are signs of our immortal souls.

God wants to share his very life with us. He does this in a powerful and visible way through the sacramental celebrations of the Church. Sacraments include visible signs and actions by people and invisible actions by God. Because we as humans perceive and understand the world in physical terms, God gives us physical signs to help us understand what is happening spiritually. God performs the real work in a sacramental celebration, but we cooperate with that work of God through our own actions. The rituals of sacramental celebrations make the invisible work of God visible to us.

Baptism, confirmation, and the Eucharist are called "sacraments of initiation" because they are the celebrations by which one enters into the life of the Church. Reconciliation and the anointing of the sick are called "sacraments of healing," because they are signs of God's healing of body and soul. Matrimony and holy orders are called "sacraments at the service of Holy Communion" because they are "directed towards the salvation of others" (*Catechism of the Catholic Church*, 1534).

BAPTISM AND ITS RELATIONSHIP TO RECONCILIATION

In the sacrament of baptism, we enter into the "paschal mystery" of Christ. In other words, we are spiritually joined to Christ's death, burial, and resurrection. In the celebration of the sacrament, we die to sin, are buried with Christ, and are raised up to live a new life in Christ (see Romans 6:3-4). The individual being baptized is immersed in water (or water is poured over his or her head) with the words "I baptize you in the name of the Father, and of the Son, and of the Holy Spirit." The baptized is then anointed with blessed oil, called "chrism." This signifies the gift of the Holy Spirit and the reality that all of us who have put on Christ in baptism share in his work as priest, prophet, and King: We are called to serve and to proclaim the Word of God, and we are adopted sons and daughters of the king, making us part of the royal family. A white garment is usually placed on the newly baptized, signifying the truth that he or she has put on Christ and is now free from the stain of sin. A baptismal candle is lit from the Easter candle (which represents Christ), showing that the newly baptized has received the light of Christ and is welcomed into the Church to participate with her in being the "light of the world."

KNOW IT • TEACH IT • SHARE IT

In summary, when we are baptized, we are adopted into God's family, the Church. We are forgiven of our sins, and we are given a mission — to act as Christ in the world. Each of these gifts also relates to the sacrament of reconciliation. When we sin, we fail to live up to the mission to which we are called by our baptism, and we need to be reconciled with our Father and our brothers and sisters. The forgiveness we receive at baptism is like a gift we can unwrap again and again through the sacrament of reconciliation. We can approach God in this way because we have been given the rights of sons and daughters through our baptism in Christ.

HOW CHILDREN UNDERSTAND THE SACRAMENTS

As concrete thinkers, young children have little understanding of an "invisible spiritual world." They *can* learn that God is with us in many ways, even though we can't see him. Children need to know that God is present in the world, and not just "up in heaven," because this understanding of God's presence is part of the basis of our sacramental theology as Catholics. It follows from God's invisible presence in the world that God also *does* things we cannot see. When we discuss sacraments with children, it's helpful to describe them as "special celebrations" in which we do some things and God does some things, explaining that the things we do and the things God does go together. An example of this is the transubstantiation of the bread and wine into the Body and Blood of Christ in the Eucharist. The priest doesn't change the bread and the wine into Jesus' Body and Blood, as if he has some special powers. Rather, God works with the priest's words and actions to simultaneously change our gifts into Christ.

In the sacrament of baptism, the sign of the pouring of water — which makes our bodies clean — demonstrates that baptism makes our souls clean of sin. Signs such as the pouring of water are not only reminders, however. God chooses to act through these actions of ours. So as the water is poured, sins are cleansed, but it's God who is doing that. We are cooperating with his work. The white baptismal garment also reminds us of this important truth. The oil reminds us that those who are baptized are *anointed* — called and chosen by God for a special purpose. We receive a baptismal candle to remind us that we have received the light of Christ and are called to carry that light into the world.

We can explain to children that Jesus gave us things we can see in sacramental celebrations so we would know how God is working in our lives at these special times — the pouring of water, the anointing with oil, the clothing with the baptismal garment, and the lighting of the baptismal candle. Though we can't see it, at the same time God is adding the person being baptized to his family, cleansing his or her soul of sin, and giving him or her a "special job" to be like Christ in the world.

It's also important to communicate to children that God gives us grace through the sacraments. It's very difficult to adequately define for young children an abstract concept such as "grace." One simple definition is "the ability God gives us to do what he has asked us to do." This is an inadequate definition, but one that conveys some important truths about God's grace. Children also must be taught that we grow in our understanding of what God is doing in the sacraments. When they are adults, they hopefully will understand the sacraments even more deeply.

Baptism and Other Sacraments

Introducing Sacraments

MAIN POINT

This activity is designed to introduce the word "sacrament." A sacrament is a special celebration of the Church in which we see signs of God's presence. It is also a way God works in us and gives us the grace to do what he asks of us.

MATERIALS NEEDED

❑ chalkboard and chalk or flip chart and marker

PREPARATION

Draw nine short, blank lines on the chalkboard or flip chart (one for each letter of the word "sacrament").

INSTRUCTIONS

With much fanfare and excitement, announce to the children that today they will learn a new word that will be very important in their lives as Catholic Christians. Invite the children to raise their hands if they would like to guess the letters that go in the blank spaces. If they name a letter that is in the word, write that letter in the appropriate space. If children name letters that are not in the puzzle, write those off to the side. Even if the children already know the word, ask them to name letters until the puzzle is completed. When the complete word is on the board, invite the children to say the word "sacrament" together, then explain that a sacrament is a special celebration. Ask the children about special celebrations they have in their own families and at school. Explain that sacraments are the special celebrations of our Church family. Tell the children that "in a sacrament, there are things that we do that tell us God is also working. God gives us grace through the sacraments. Grace is the ability God gives us to do the things he asks us to do."

Seven Sacraments Guessing Game

MAIN POINT

This activity is designed to teach children the names of the seven sacraments and what distinguishes one from another.

MATERIALS NEEDED

- ❑ Reproducible: "Seven Sacraments Guessing Game — Question Cards"
- ❑ Reproducible: "Seven Sacraments Guessing Game — Answer Cards"
- ❑ seven envelopes
- ❑ one pair of scissors
- ❑ one bottle of glue

PREPARATION

Make one copy of "Seven Sacraments Guessing Game— Question Cards" and "Seven Sacraments Guessing Game — Answer Cards." Cut out the clues and answers. Glue one clue on the front of each envelope. Inside each envelope, place the correct answer.

INSTRUCTIONS

After a brief overview of all seven sacraments (which may be a part of your usual curriculum), announce that you will now play a guessing game about the sacraments. Explain to the children that you will read a clue, then ask them to guess which sacrament you are talking about. Read the clue, and invite the kids to raise their hands if they know the answer. Call on a child with his or her hand raised, and after the child responds, hand the envelope to him or her and ask him or her to open it and read the answer. Continue until you have used all seven envelopes.

1. This sacrament welcomes people into God's family.

2. This sacrament reminds us that God loves us no matter what.

3. In this sacrament, Jesus is truly and completely present — Body and Blood, Soul and Divinity.

4. People who are very sick celebrate this sacrament. It is a special prayer for healing.

5. In this sacrament, we are sealed with the Holy Spirit. The Spirit begins to work in us in a special way.

6. In this sacrament, a man and a woman make a special promise to love and care for each other forever.

7. In this sacrament, men promise to serve the Church as priests or deacons.

1. Baptism

2. Reconciliation

3. Eucharist

4. Anointing of the Sick

5. Confirmation

6. Matrimony (Marriage)

7. Holy Orders

My Baptismal Story

MAIN POINT

By researching their baptism, children begin to claim the baptism as their own, and they have an opportunity to connect their baptism with the sacrament of reconciliation.

MATERIALS NEEDED

- ❏ Reproducible: "My Baptismal Story"
- ❏ pencils or pens
- ❏ crayons

PREPARATION

Make one copy of "My Baptismal Story" for each child in your group. You may wish to send this sheet home to parents the week before you will use it, or ask parents to talk to their children about their baptism, so the kids will have details they can write in their booklets.

INSTRUCTIONS

Ask the children if they have ever seen a baptism. Ask them what they saw, and ask them what they know about their own baptisms. Assist the children in folding "My Baptismal Story" so it forms a booklet. Help them write about their baptisms in their booklets. (If you have little or no details, help them write things that are true for all baptisms, such as, "There was water," "I was added to God's family.") The children also may wish to color their booklets.

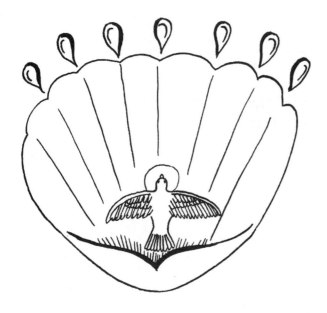

Renewing the Promises of Baptism

MAIN POINT

When we are baptized, we make promises (or our parents make promises for us) to avoid sin and live as Christian people. We can renew those promises as we grow in knowledge of what God asks us to do and as we grow in his grace.

MATERIALS NEEDED

- ❑ baptismal font
- ❑ candles (one for each child)
- ❑ larger candle
- ❑ matches or lighter
- ❑ Reproducible: "Baptismal Promises"

PREPARATION

Set up the large candle near the baptismal font, and place the smaller candles for the children nearby. Make one copy of "Baptismal Promises" for your own reference.

INSTRUCTIONS

Gather the children in a circle around the baptismal font. Explain that when people are baptized, they make promises to avoid sin and live as Christian people. If we are very young, our parents make those promises for us, but when we are more able to understand the difference between right and wrong, we can make those promises, too. Ask the children to listen closely as you read the baptismal promises and to answer "I do" to show their agreement. Read each question on "Baptismal Promises." Next, ask the children to bless themselves with holy water from the font. Finally, light each of the small candles, one by one, handing one to each of the children as it is lit. As you give each child a candle, say, "(Child's Name), receive the light of Christ." When everyone has a candle, pray this closing prayer:

"Dear God, you gave the light of Christ to each one of us at our baptism. Help us to take Christ's light into the world through the things we do and say. Amen"

Baptismal Promises

Do you reject sin, so as to live in the freedom of God's children?

I do.

Do you reject the glamor of evil, and refuse to be mastered by sin?

I do.

Do you reject Satan, father of sin and prince of darkness?

I do.

Do you believe in God, the Father Almighty,
    creator of heaven and earth?

I do.

Do you believe in Jesus Christ, his only Son, our Lord,
    who was born of the Virgin Mary,
    was crucified, died, and was buried,
    rose from the dead, and is now seated at the right hand of the Father?

I do.

Do you believe in the Holy Spirit,
    the holy catholic Church, the communion of saints,
    the forgiveness of sins, the resurrection of the body,
    and life everlasting?

I do.

This is our faith. This is the faith of the Church. We are proud to profess it, in Christ Jesus our Lord.

Amen.

Baptism and Other Sacraments

Dear Parents,

Our topic now is sacraments. A sacrament is a special Church celebration in which God is present. In every sacramental celebration, people perform some actions, and God performs others. Sacraments give us grace; through the sacraments, God increases our ability to do what he asks of us.

There are seven sacraments. Baptism, confirmation, and the Eucharist are called "sacraments of initiation" because they are the celebrations by which one enters into the life of the Church. Reconciliation and anointing of the sick, signs of God's healing of body and soul, are called "sacraments of healing." Matrimony and holy orders are called "sacraments at the service of Holy Communion" because they are "directed towards the salvation of others" (*Catechism of the Catholic Church*, 1534).

Baptism is the sacrament through which we are welcomed into God's family, the Church, and freed from the stain of sin. The forgiveness we receive at baptism is a gift we can open again and again through the sacrament of reconciliation. We can approach God as his child in the sacrament of reconciliation because when we were baptized, God adopted us as his own sons and daughters. What an incredible gift! Because of baptism's relationship to the other sacraments we celebrate, it is helpful for children to learn more about baptism when preparing for the sacrament of reconciliation. Many children, baptized as infants, don't remember their baptism, but parents can help by showing them pictures and other mementos and talking about their own memories of that special day.

This week, please spend some time talking with your child about his or her baptism and what you remember. Also discuss other special times in your family's life when you feel God's presence with you.

God Bless,

Estimados padres de familia,

Nuestro tema ahora es los sacramentos. El sacramento es una celebración especial de la Iglesia en la cual Dios esta presente. En toda celebración sacramental la gente realiza algunas acciones, y Dios realiza otras. Los sacramentos nos dan gracia; por medio de los sacramentos, Dios aumenta nuestra habilidad para hacer lo que él nos manda.

Hay siete sacramentos. El bautismo, la confirmación, y la Eucaristía son llamados "los sacramentos de iniciación" porque son las celebraciones por medio de las cuales uno entra dentro de la vida de la Iglesia. La reconciliación y la unción de los enfermos señales de que Dios sana el cuerpo y el alma, son llamados "sacramentos sanativos." El matrimonio y la orden sacerdotal son llamados "los sacramentos al servicio de la Sagrada Comunión" porque están "dirigidos hacia la salvación de otros" (*Catechism of the Catholic Church,* 1534).

El bautismo es el sacramento por medio del cual somos bienvenidos dentro de la familia de Dios, la Iglesia, y librados de la mancha del pecado. El perdón que recibimos en el bautismo es un regalo que podemos abrir una y otra vez a través del sacramento de la reconciliación. Nos podemos acercar a Dios como su hijo en el sacramento de la reconciliación porque cuando fuimos bautizados, Dios nos adoptó como sus propios hijos e hijas. ¡Qué regalo más increíble! Debido a la relación del bautismo con los otros sacramentos que celebramos, es una ayuda para los niños que aprendan más sobre el bautismo cuando se están preparando para el sacramento de la reconciliación. Muchos niños bautizados cuando son infantes, generalmente no se acuerdan de su bautismo, pero los papás les pueden ayudar a recordar mostrándoles fotos y otros recuerdos y hablándoles sobre sus propios recuerdos de ese día tan especial.

Esta semana, por favor pasen un tiempo hablando con su hijo o hija sobre su bautismo y de lo que usted se acuerda. También hable sobre otros momentos especiales en la vida de su familia cuando usted siente la presencia de Dios con usted.

Que Dios los Bendiga,

Forgiveness

In the Old Testament book of Jonah, we read about the city of Ninevah — a city that had strayed so far that God said, "their wickedness has come up before me" (Jonah 1:2). God sends Jonah to Ninevah so the people of the city may be warned of the tragedy that will befall them if they do not repent. Jonah is reluctant at first and tries to run from God's call. He gets himself into some serious trouble; but God delivers him, keeps him safe, and again asks him to go to Ninevah. When Jonah arrives in the big city, he begins to spread God's message. Immediately, the people of the city respond. They realize the wrong they have done and begin to pray and fast. The king sends out a decree that everyone in the city should fast and pray for God's mercy. God sees their contrition and forgives their sins. Ninevah is saved. Jonah later proclaims that God is "a gracious God and merciful, slow to anger, and abounding in steadfast love" (Jonah 4:2).

The story of Ninevah illustrates two important points about God's forgiveness. First, it begins with God. God initiated Ninevah's reconciliation with himself. He sent Jonah as a sign to call the people to repentance. In a similar way, God initiates our reconciliation to himself through his grace and the work of the Holy Spirit. Second, God hears and is touched by our contrition. He gives us opportunity to repent and is moved when we do. In his compassion, he restores us.

Scripture offers many other examples of forgiveness and reconciliation. In John 4:1-42, Scripture tells us how Jesus revealed himself to the woman at the well, a sinful woman shunned by others. She immediately shared the message of Christ with others, which provided some common ground between the woman and her community. In a sense, then, Jesus not only forgave the woman her sins but also reintegrated her into the community. The sacrament of reconciliation has these same effects for us today: Through the sacrament we are forgiven of our sin and united once again with Christ and his Church.

In Luke 7:36-50, we read that while Jesus is dining at the house of a Pharisee, a woman known by the others to be very sinful (probably a prostitute) enters the house. She is weeping and washes Jesus' feet with her tears. She then anoints his feet with expensive, sweet-smelling oil. The Pharisee is very troubled by the woman's presence and is particularly appalled that Jesus is allowing such a sinful woman to touch him. Jesus answers this concern with a parable about a creditor who forgives a large debt, saying that those who have been forgiven much will show great love. Jesus teaches that no sin is too large to be forgiven. We can always bring our failures to God.

Because God has shown us love and mercy, we should also be willing to love and show mercy to one another. In the Lord's Prayer, we ask God to "forgive us our trespasses as we forgive those who trespass against us." Jesus said, "if you forgive men their trespasses, your heavenly Father also will forgive you" (Matthew 6:14). Our ability to receive God's gift of forgiveness depends in part on our openness to share that gift with others.

HOW CHILDREN UNDERSTAND FORGIVENESS

Most children have an idea of what it means to forgive. In fact, children are sometimes better at forgiving than we adults. For children, however, forgiveness is sometimes reduced to the simple cliché "forgive and forget." God commands us to forgive those who have wronged us, but he doesn't command us to always forget, particularly if forgetting means that we would make ourselves vulnerable to being hurt. Forgiving does not mean letting others walk all over you, because God wants us to show respect for ourselves as well.

When explaining forgiveness to children, it may be helpful to ask them about times when it is hard to forgive. Let them know that God understands this and will give them help in forgiving others if they ask him to. Talk, too, about the difference between forgiving and letting someone take advantage of them. Reassure them that forgiving doesn't always mean completely trusting again, but it does mean leaving justice or vengeance to God, not holding grudges or nursing our anger.

TEACH IT

Forgiveness

The Gift of God's Forgiveness

MAIN POINT

God gives us his gift of forgiveness when we are baptized. Forgiveness is like a present we can open again and again through the sacrament of reconciliation.

MATERIALS NEEDED

- ❑ empty box with a lid (shoe box or dress-shirt box)
- ❑ gift wrap
- ❑ scissors
- ❑ ribbon
- ❑ tape
- ❑ index card or piece of paper with the word "forgiveness" printed on it

PREPARATION

Place the paper or card on which you have written the word "forgiveness" inside a small box. Wrap the box like a gift with wrapping paper and ribbon. (You may wish to wrap the lid separately so the package can be reused.)

INSTRUCTIONS

Tell the children you have a gift you would like to share with them. Take out the gift and wonder aloud what might be in the box. Open the box and show the children the word on the card inside. Talk about what "forgiveness" means. Explain to the children that one of the gifts we receive at baptism is forgiveness from our sins. We still sometimes sin after baptism, however. God makes this forgiveness available to us again and again through the sacrament of reconciliation.

The Prodigal Son

MAIN POINT

God always forgives us and welcomes us back. He loves us no matter what.

MATERIALS NEEDED

- ❑ Two Bible-time costumes (such as large pieces of fabric with rope for belts, robes, etc.)
- ❑ Men's suit jacket and tie or women's suit jacket (from a thrift store or the closet at home)
- ❑ Pretend microphone (a toy microphone or one made out of an empty toilet paper roll with a foam ball or ping-pong ball on top)
- ❑ Reproducible: "The Prodigal Son"

PREPARATION

Make three copies of "The Prodigal Son."

INSTRUCTIONS

Briefly tell the parable of the prodigal son using a children's book or similar resource. Next, choose children to play the parts of the newscaster, the prodigal son, and the father. Give each of the actors a copy of the script and a costume, and give the microphone to the newscaster. Ask the children to follow the lines and motions of the script. (You may wish to give them an opportunity to practice in the hallway or an adjoining room before performing the play in front of the class.)

The Prodigal Son

Newscaster: Hello, I'm (Your Name) from W-O-R-D, Jerusalem News. I'm standing beside a road just a few miles outside the city, where I am told the prodigal son will be walking in just a few minutes. Oh, there he is now! Excuse me, sir. Do you mind if I ask you a few questions?

Prodigal Son: Go right ahead! But you'll have to walk with me. I'm sort of in a hurry.

Newscaster: Well, I heard you were leaving the city now that you are out of money. Is that true? Where are you going?

Prodigal Son: I'm going back to my father's house. I left there a few months ago with my share of his money. I told my father I didn't want to be with him anymore and that I was going out to have a good time.

Newscaster: So what brings you back home?

Prodigal Son: Well, I ran out of money, and my so-called friends didn't want to have anything to do with me anymore. I had to get a job so I could have something to eat, but the only job I could find was taking care of pigs, and I had to eat their feed.

Newscaster: Yuck, that sounds terrible!

Prodigal Son: It was. I remembered that even my father's servants lived much better than that, so I'm going back to ask him if I can at least be a servant in his house. I don't think he could ever call me "son" again after what I did.

Newscaster: And we're nearing the father's house now . . . I can see someone standing outside the house . . . Could it be? Yes, it is! The father appears to be watching for the son. And now he has seen us and is running this way! This is amazing! Apparently the father was hoping his son would come back and was watching for him just in case.

(The father and son run toward each other and hug.)

Father: Son, I'm so glad you're back. Welcome home!

Son: I'm not worthy to be called your son; make me one of your servants.

Father: Nonsense! We're going to celebrate that my son has returned.

Newscaster: Excuse me, Mr. Father, but are you saying that you're not even angry at your son? You're going to take him back just like that? And have a party, too?

Father: Why shouldn't I celebrate? My son was lost, and now he is found! This is a happy day indeed!

Forgiveness Letter

MAIN POINT

God says we should forgive others, even when they make us angry or sad. Letting go of our angry feelings is not always easy, but it can help us feel happier and be more ready to accept God's gift of forgiveness.

MATERIALS NEEDED

- ❑ Reproducible: "Forgiveness Letter"
- ❑ pen or pencil
- ❑ scissors (one pair for each child)

PREPARATION

Make a copy of "Forgiveness Letter" for each child in the class.

INSTRUCTIONS

Explain to the children that God asks us to forgive others, just as he forgives us. Give each child a copy of "Forgiveness Letter." Ask the kids to think of someone who has made them angry or upset, then complete the bottom portion of the letter. Let the kids know they don't *have* to give the letters to the people they wrote them to, but it might promote some peace and healing if they are still having trouble getting along with that person.

Forgiveness Letter

Think about a time you felt angry with someone close to you, such as a friend or family member. Write or draw what happened:

God says we should forgive others, even when they make us angry or sad. Letting go of our angry feelings is not always easy, but it can help us feel happier and be more ready to accept God's gift of forgiveness. Complete this forgiveness letter. You may even choose to give the letter to the person you felt angry with.

Dear _____,

I felt _____ when _____

_____,

but I forgive you, because _____

_____. I hope we can be friends again.

Sincerely,

SHARE IT

Forgiveness

Dear Parents,

Scripture is full of examples of God's forgiveness. Jesus himself gave many examples of God's mercy, both in the parables he told and in the way he reached out even to those who were known to be sinful. The following are some important points we can learn from Christ about forgiveness:

- God initiates our reconciliation to himself through his grace and the work of the Holy Spirit.
- God hears and is touched by our contrition. He gives us the opportunity to repent and is moved when we do.
- In his mercy, God forgives our sin and reunites us with his family, the Church.
- No sin is so large that it cannot be forgiven. We can always bring our failures to God.
- Because of the love and mercy God has shown us, we also should be willing to forgive and show mercy to one another. Jesus said, "If you forgive men their trespasses, your heavenly Father also will forgive you" (Matthew 6:14).

Forgiving isn't always easy, but forgiving isn't the same as forgetting. It means not holding on to our anger, letting go of our grudges, and leaving justice to God.

All families have conflicts sometimes. The next time there is a disagreement in your family, use it as an opportunity to talk about God's forgiveness and what Jesus said about forgiving others. When we allow ourselves to forgive, we are more ready to accept God's forgiveness, and we spread the peace of Christ in the world.

God Bless,

COMPÁRTALO

El Perdón

KNOW IT • TEACH IT • COMPÁRTALO

FORGIVENESS 87

Estimados padres de familia,

La Sagrada Escritura está llena de ejemplos del perdón de Dios. Jesús mismo dio muchos ejemplos de la misericordia de Dios, tanto en las parábolas que contó como en la manera en que tendió la mano inclusive hacia aquellos quienes eran conocidos como pecadores. Los siguientes son algunos puntos importantes que podemos aprender de Cristo sobre el perdón:

- Dios inicia nuestra reconciliación hacia él mismo a través de su gracia y el trabajo del Espíritu Santo.
- Dios oye y es conmovido por nuestra contrición. Él nos da la oportunidad de arrepentirnos, y se conmueve cuando lo hacemos.
- En su misericordia, Dios perdona nuestro pecado y nos reúne con su familia, la Iglesia.
- Ningún pecado es tan grande que no puede ser perdonado. Siempre podemos llevar nuestras faltas a Dios.
- Por el amor y la misericordia que Dios nos ha demostrado, también debemos estar dispuestos a perdonar y a demostrar misericordia el uno al otro. Jesús dijo, "Si ustedes perdonan a los hombres sus ofensas, también el Padre celestial les perdonará a ustedes" (San Mateo 6:14).

Perdonar no es fácil siempre, pero perdonar no es lo mismo que olvidar. Significa no guardar dentro nuestro coraje, soltar nuestros rencores, y dejar la justicia a Dios.

Todas las familias tienen a veces conflictos. La próxima vez que haya un desacuerdo en su familia, utilícelo como una oportunidad para hablar sobre el perdón de Dios y lo que Jesús dijo sobre perdonar a los demás. Cuando estamos dispuestos a perdonar, estamos más listos para aceptar el perdón de Dios y repartimos la paz de Cristo en el Mundo.

Que Dios los Bendiga,

The Sacrament of Reconciliation, Part I

The Sacrament of Reconciliation, Part I

For many adults, discussion of the sacrament of reconciliation, or "confession," evokes feelings of anxiety. We may picture dark, foreboding confessionals or remember feelings of shame or guilt associated with our experiences of confession in childhood. In recent years, the Church has worked to change both the form of and instruction on this sacrament to make it the positive experience of unconditional love that God intends it to be. First and foremost, reconciliation should be a powerful reminder that God loves us "no matter what." It is a tangible sign of God's desire to reach out to us, even in our sinfulness, to help us reconcile ourselves with him and our brothers and sisters and repair the damage done by sin.

Sin disrupts our relationship with God and with the community. Jesus illustrated the communal aspect of forgiveness when he forgave those who had alienated themselves from others, such as Zacchaeus the tax collector and Mary the penitent, and helped them rejoin the community (*Catechism of the Catholic Church,* 1443). In the Rite of Reconciliation, the priest represents both Christ and the Christian community, a sign of the restoration of our relationship with God and our fellowship with one another.

The Catechism of the Catholic Church (1448) describes two major elements of the sacrament of reconciliation: *our actions* and *God's actions.* Our actions consist of *contrition,* or feeling truly sorry for our sin; *confession* of our sin to the priest; and *satisfaction*: doing what we can to repair the damage resulting from our sin. God's actions in the sacrament include restoring us to his grace and reconciling us to himself and to the Church.

THE SIGN OF THE CROSS

Celebration of the sacrament of reconciliation begins, as all sacramental celebrations do, with the Sign of the Cross. This conveys the powerful truth that something more than what we can see is happening. God is present, and the actions of the sacrament will be performed in his name. God is Father, our loving parent, provider, and guide. God is Son, our brother, in solidarity with us. God is Holy Spirit, the very breath we breathe, the Life Force that sustains us physically and spiritually. Realization of each of these three persons in one God is vital in our celebration of the sacrament.

We come with contrition for abandoning our Father's guidance, but with the knowledge that we can approach him because we have been adopted as brothers and sisters of the Son. We are brought here to be reconciled by the Spirit, who has worked in our hearts to help us come to contrition, and who will guide us through reconciliation and help us make better choices if we listen to his voice.

WELCOMED IN PEACE

The Rite of Reconciliation continues with the welcome of the priest, who proclaims peace to us in the name of Jesus and the Christian community. No matter what we have done, we are always welcome to come back to Christ and to his family, the Church. The priest's welcome is a visible sign of this truth. The welcome may be simple and short, or it may include a passage from Scripture designed to help us more fully appreciate what is about to happen.

CONFESSION OF SIN

Confident that God welcomes and hears us, we bring our burdens, struggles, and failures to him. The priest's active listening is a sign that God is listening to what is on our hearts. Making a good confession requires some humility and a thorough examination of conscience. When confessing sins, it is generally considered appropriate to name the categories of sin that one wishes to confess and perhaps some specific instances, but there is no need to mention each occurrence of venial sin in a "laundry list" format.

HOW CHILDREN UNDERSTAND THE SACRAMENT OF RECONCILIATION

For some Catholic children, the sacrament of reconciliation is cloaked in mystery. They have never heard what is being said when the sacrament is celebrated, and if they haven't been to a communal penance service, they may not have seen the sacrament, either. Going step-by-step through the actions helps put children at ease and frees them to focus on what the actions mean, rather than whether it will be scary or difficult, or whatever else they may imagine. It's important that we as catechists be familiar enough with the rite to be able to explain it accurately and fully. The following pages will provide some tips for teaching both the meaning and the practical aspects of the basic steps of the rite.

The Sacrament of Reconciliation, Part I

Class Photo Mural: Jesus Welcomes the Children

MAIN POINT

Jesus loves each of us and welcomes us to meet him in the sacrament of reconciliation.

MATERIALS NEEDED

- ❑ individual photo of each child in the group
- ❑ masking tape
- ❑ poster of Jesus with arms outstretched (or homemade drawing of Jesus on poster board or large piece of paper)

PREPARATION

Ask the children's parents to send a small photo of each child to be used on a class mural (or take the photos yourself with parents' permission). Put the poster or drawing of Jesus on one of the walls in the room, within the children's reach.

INSTRUCTIONS

Sit in a circle with the children. Make sure each child has his or her photo in hand. Talk about how Jesus loves each of us and welcomes us all to meet him in the sacrament of reconciliation. You may wish to highlight his particular love for all children, as shown in Matthew 19:13-14. Call on the children individually, asking them to tape their picture to the poster of Jesus as a sign of his welcoming them to the sacrament of reconciliation.

Holy Trinity: Who Am I?

MAIN POINT

God's name tells us about who God is. We begin the sacrament of reconciliation in the name of the Father, Son, and Holy Spirit, and each person of God is present with us in the sacrament.

MATERIALS NEEDED

- ❑ Reproducibles: "Holy Trinity: Who Am I?" Questions and Answers
- ❑ nine envelopes
- ❑ one bottle of glue
- ❑ one pair of scissors
- ❑ holy cards featuring pictures that represent God the Father, Jesus, and the Holy Spirit (optional)

PREPARATION

Cut out the clues and answers on "Holy Trinity: Who Am I?" Questions and Answers. Paste a numbered clue on the outside of each envelope. Inside each envelope, place the correct answer, using either the answer pictures or holy cards that represent the Father, Son, and Holy Spirit.

INSTRUCTIONS

Remind the children that there are three persons in the one God — the Father, the Son, and the Holy Spirit. Explain to them that you will be playing a game with envelopes that contain the names of the three persons of God. They will try to guess which name is in each envelope from the clues on the outside. Read each clue and invite the kids to raise their hands if they know the answer. Call on a child with his or her hand raised, and after the child responds, ask him or her to open the envelope and read the answer. Continue until you have used all nine envelopes.

One day, I came down to earth as a mighty wind and tongues of fire.

I live in the hearts of all Christians, and I help them make right choices.

I come to you in a special way when you are baptized and when you are confirmed

I came to earth as a little baby.

I lived on the earth for about thirty-three years.

I died on a cross, but rose from the dead three days later.

I created everything.

I take care of all living things.

Jesus prayed to me the night before he died.

Holy Trinity: Who Am I? — Answers

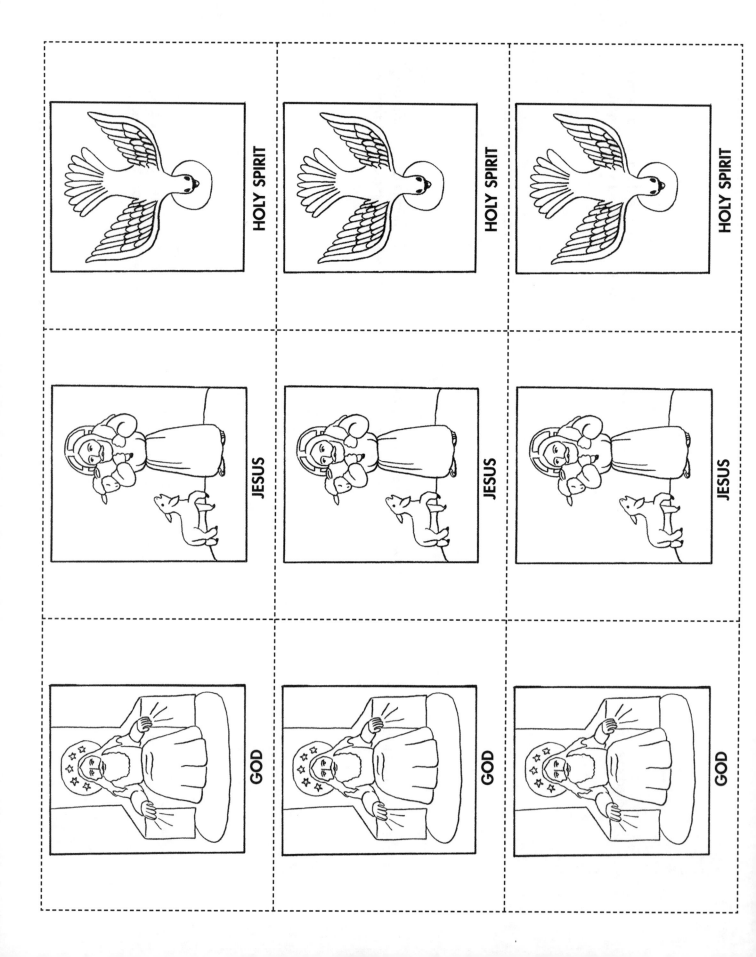

I'm Sorry

MAIN POINT

Naming what we have done wrong is the first step in saying "I'm sorry" and becoming friends again.

MATERIALS NEEDED

- ❏ Reproducible: "I'm Sorry Letter"
- ❏ pens or pencils

PREPARATION

Make a copy of "I'm Sorry Letter" for each child.

INSTRUCTIONS

Tell the children that God expects us to admit the wrong we have done and say "I'm sorry." This can help others know we care about how they feel and help us begin to be friends again. Ask them to first think of something they have done that they might want to say "I'm sorry" for. (Some children may benefit from examples, such as "not following your mom or dad's directions," "losing your temper with your brother, sister, or friend," or "misbehaving in class at school.") Ask the kids to think of whom they might have hurt with their actions, then write or draw what happened and write a letter.

I'm Sorry Letter

Think about a time when you made someone feel sad or angry. Write or draw what happened:

When we make someone feel angry or hurt because we have broken one of God's rules, we should admit what we have done and let the person know we are sorry. This is the first step toward becoming friends again. Complete the "I'm Sorry" letter below. You may choose to give this letter to the person you hurt.

Dear _____,

I'm really sorry about the time I _____

_____ .

You probably felt _____

when I did that. I hope we can be friends again.

Sincerely,

The Sacrament of Reconciliation, Part I

Dear Parents,

Today we had the first of our lessons on celebrating the sacrament of reconciliation. For many adults, discussion of the sacrament of reconciliation, or "confession," evokes feelings of anxiety. We may picture dark, foreboding confessionals or remember feelings of shame or guilt associated with our experiences of confession in childhood. In recent years, the Church has worked to change both form and instruction in this sacrament to make it the positive experience of unconditional love that God intends it to be. First and foremost, reconciliation should be a powerful reminder that God loves us no matter what. It is a tangible sign of God's desire to reach out to us, even in our sinfulness, to help us reconcile ourselves with him and with our brothers and sisters and to repair the damage resulting from our sin.

Celebration of the sacrament of reconciliation begins, as all sacramental celebrations do, with the Sign of the Cross. We are then welcomed by the priest, who proclaims peace to us in the name of Jesus and the Christian community. No matter what we have done, we are always welcome to come back to Christ and to his family, the Church. Confident that God welcomes and hears us, we bring our burdens, struggles, and failures to him. The priest's active listening is a sign that God is listening to what is in our hearts.

For some Catholic children, the sacrament of reconciliation is cloaked in mystery. They have never heard what is being said when the sacrament is celebrated, and they may not have seen the sacrament, either. Parents can help by familiarizing themselves with the form of the sacrament and the theology behind it. If you have been away from the sacrament for a while, consider meeting Jesus in reconciliation once again. Children can also benefit from attending the parishwide penance services typically held during Advent and Lent. This gives them the opportunity to see what celebration of the sacrament looks like and may reduce the anxiety sometimes associated with the unknown. May God bless you and your family as you prepare your child to experience this important reminder of God's unconditional love.

Sincerely,

El Sacramento de la Reconciliación, 1ra Parte

Estimados Padres de Familia,

Hoy tuvimos la primera de nuestras lecciones sobre la celebración del sacramento de la reconciliación. Para muchos adultos, hablar sobre el sacramento de la reconciliación, o "confesión," evoca sentimientos de ansiedad. Nos imaginamos confesionarios oscuros, o recordamos sentimientos de vergüenza o culpabilidad asociados con nuestras experiencias con la confesión en nuestra niñez. En años recientes, la Iglesia ha trabajado para cambiar la forma y la enseñanza de este sacramento para hacerla como es la intención de Dios, una experiencia positiva de amor incondicional. Lo primero y lo principal, la reconciliación debe ser un poderoso recordatorio de que Dios nos ama pase lo que pase. Es una señal tangible del deseo de Dios de tendernos la mano, inclusive en nuestra maldad, para ayudarnos a reconciliarnos nosotros mismos con él y con nuestros hermanos y hermanas y reparar el daño resultante de nuestro pecado.

La celebración del sacramento de la reconciliación comienza como toda celebración sacramental, con la Señal de La Cruz. Entonces el sacerdote nos da la bienvenida, quien nos proclama la paz en el nombre de Jesús y la comunidad Cristiana. No importa lo que hayamos hecho, siempre somos bienvenidos para regresar a Cristo y a su familia, la Iglesia. Confiados en que Dios nos da la bienvenida y nos escucha, le traemos a él nuestras cargas, nuestras luchas, y nuestros fracasos. Cuando el sacerdote nos escucha activamente esta es una señal de que Dios está escuchando lo que traemos en nuestros corazones.

Para algunos niños Católicos, el sacramento de la reconciliación es una capa de misterio. Ellos nunca han escuchado lo que se dice cuando se celebra este sacramento, y posiblemente no han visto el sacramento tampoco. Los padres de familia pueden ayudar al familiarizarse con la forma del sacramento y la teología detrás de él. Si usted ha estado alejado del sacramento por algún tiempo, considere reunirse una vez más con Jesús en la reconciliación. Los niños también pueden beneficiarse asistiendo a los servicios de penitencia en la parroquia los cuales toman lugar típicamente durante el tiempo de adviento y de la cuaresma. Esto les da la oportunidad de ver lo que es la celebración de este sacramento y les puede reducir la ansiedad a veces asociada con lo desconocido. Que Dios lo bendiga a usted y a su familia al preparar a su hijo o hija para que sientan esta experiencia que es un recordatorio importante del amor incondicional de Dios.

Sinceramente,

The Sacrament of Reconciliation, Part II

The Sacrament of Reconciliation, Part II

PENANCE

After our confession of sin, the priest gives us a *penance*, a special action to perform. It's not a way of *earning* God's forgiveness — that's a gift given freely by God.

Rather, it's an act to help us repair the damage to our souls or to relationships. Doing penance helps us show more fully our contrition for sin and helps us grow in holiness. The penance may include doing something nice for someone we have wronged, taking up a good habit, or saying a special prayer. Sometimes the penance we are given in the sacrament of reconciliation involves more than one of the above. As part of this step, we also pray an Act of Contrition, a prayer of sorrow for our sins.

ABSOLUTION

After the penitent confesses and the priest gives the penance, the priest says the words of absolution. These words remind us of several important truths (see *Catechism of the Catholic Church*, 1449): (1) God the Father is the source of forgiveness; (2) God reconciles us with himself through the death and resurrection of Jesus and through the Holy Spirit; (3) God chooses the Church as the vehicle through which he gives his gift of forgiveness. When the priest says the words of absolution, God forgives all our sins, and we are reconciled with him and with the Church. This is truly a joyous moment!

THE CONCLUSION OF THE RITE

The Rite of Reconciliation ends with a prayer of thanksgiving and praise and the blessing of the priest. We are sent forth, reconciled with God and our brothers and sisters, to spread the peace we have received. Often in the Gospels, when Jesus heals individuals, they spread the news of the great things he has done. We, too, should spread the joy of what God has done for us by sharing him with others. We share him by our example and by our words. We spread his message of reconciliation by forgiving others and being peacemakers.

HOW CHILDREN UNDERSTAND THE SACRAMENT OF RECONCILIATION

Young children can easily understand the concepts of contrition and penance as "showing that you're sorry" and "trying to make up for what you have done wrong."

KNOW IT ● TEACH IT ● SHARE IT

They find more abstract the concept that penance also works to repair sin's damage to our own souls. Penance helps us grow as children of God, becoming more like Christ in our actions. It is helpful to give children some idea of what a penance might be. You may say that a child who confesses to making fun of a peer at school may be asked to do something nice for that peer. A child who confesses to disobeying his or her parents may be asked to help Mom or Dad with the housework without asking. A penance might also (and usually does) involve a prayer. You can explain to children that praying the prayers given to us as penance helps us grow in our relationship with God. Good friends talk to each other, and we talk to God through prayer. Prayer also changes our hearts by making us more open to the ways in which God leads us.

The major points of the words of absolution relate to a common protest made by children who are celebrating reconciliation for the first time: "Why do I have to confess my sins to the priest? Can't I just talk directly to God?" We can remind children that God really is the only one who forgives sin, and he is present in the sacrament of reconciliation, just as he is present in all of the sacraments. God chooses to work through the Church (and through the priest specifically) to forgive sins so we will have a sign from him of what is happening (or for children, "so we can see what God is doing"). The priest represents both Jesus and the Christian community, and when we are welcomed and forgiven by him, we know that God and the Church welcome and forgive us as well. It is truly a blessing to know this by the things we see and hear! One reason children are anxious about confessing to the priest is that they are concerned the priest will think less of them. Remind them that the priest hears sins from many different people, young and old, and there is probably nothing they could confess that he hasn't heard before. He expects them to talk about their sins, so he won't be surprised or shocked by what they say, and he can't tell anyone else about what they say because of the seal of confession.

Another way to help put children at ease is to show them the reconciliation room and role-play the steps of the rite. Try role-playing first with another adult (but have the adult "confess" things that would be relevant for a child, such as disobedience to parents, fighting with siblings, etc.). Then ask the kids to role-play with you. Remind them that this is not a real confession, and they shouldn't tell you their real sins; this is just practice to help them learn the form of the rite.

The Sacrament of Reconciliation, Part II

The Story of Zacchaeus

MAIN POINT

When we feel sorry about the wrong we have done to others, we should take steps to make it right.

MATERIALS NEEDED

- ❑ Reproducible: "Zacchaeus"
- ❑ several Bible-time costumes (long pieces of fabric, thin rope, robes, etc.)
- ❑ green and brown construction paper or poster board

PREPARATION

Make a tree by turning a chair around backwards and taping green and brown poster board to the back of the chair and chair legs. Make copies of "Zacchaeus" for each child in the group.

INSTRUCTIONS

Briefly tell the story of Zacchaeus using a children's book or similar resource. Next, choose children to play the parts of Jesus, Zacchaeus, and the crowd of people. Give each of the actors a copy of the script and a costume. Ask the children to follow the lines and motions of the script. (You may wish to give them an opportunity to practice in the hallway or an adjoining room before performing the play in front of the class.)

Zacchaeus

(Crowd of people enters, with Zacchaeus in the back)

Crowd: Jesus is coming! Jesus is coming!

Zacchaeus: I can't see anything! I'm too short to see over their heads!

Crowd: Here he comes now! He's coming this way!

Zacchaeus: I want to see Jesus! (Climbs into the "tree.")

(Jesus stops in front of the crowd because he notices Zacchaeus in the tree.)

Jesus: Zacchaeus, come down. Today, I'm coming to your house for dinner.

Crowd: Oh, no, Jesus, that man is a tax collector. He cheats people! You don't want to have dinner with him!

Jesus: Sure I do! I came to show people like him how to do what God wants.

Zacchaeus: Jesus, I'm sorry if I have cheated people. I'll give half of what I have to the poor to try to make things right.

Fill-in-the-Blank Prayers

MAIN POINT

The reproducibles that follow are prayers commonly used with the sacrament of reconciliation (the Act of Contrition and prayers commonly assigned as penance). They are meant to assist children in familiarizing themselves with these prayers.

MATERIALS NEEDED

- ❑ Reproducible: "Act of Contrition"
- ❑ Reproducible: "Our Father"
- ❑ Reproducible: "Hail Mary"
- ❑ Reproducible: "Glory Be"
- ❑ pens or pencils

PREPARATION

Make one copy of each reproducible for each child in the group.

INSTRUCTIONS

You may wish to introduce these common prayers one at a time throughout the year, rather than using them all at once. Explain to the children that the Act of Contrition is a prayer that says we are sorry and will try our hardest to do better. The other prayers are common prayers that are given as penance because when we talk to God, we grow closer to him and become friends with him again. The Act of Contrition used here is a child-friendly version. It is printed in its entirety below:

Dear God, I'm sorry for my sins with all my heart. When I chose to do wrong things and didn't do good things, I sinned against you. I should love you more than anything else. I promise to do penance and to stay away from sin and anything that leads me away from you. Amen.

Act of Contrition

Dear _____, I'm _____ for my

_____ with all my _____.

When I _____ to do wrong things,

and didn't do _____ things

I _____ against you. I should _____

you more than _____else.

I _____ to do _____ and to

stay away from _____ and anything

that _____ me away from _____.

Amen.

Our Father

Our _____, who art in _____,

hallowed be thy _____.

Thy _____ come. Thy _____ be done

on _____ as it is in _____.

Give us this _____ our daily _____,

And _____ us our trespasses,

As we _____ those who _____ against us,

And _____ us _____ into temptation,

but _____ us from _____.

Amen.

Hail Mary

Hail, _____, full of _____,

the _____ is with you.

_____ are you among

_____,

and _____is the _____ of

your womb, _____.

_____ Mary, Mother of _____,

pray for us _____,

now and at the _____ of our

_____.

Amen.

Glory Be

Glory be to the _____

and to the _____,

and to the

_____ _____.

As it was in the

_____, is _____,

and _____shall be,

_____ without _____.

Amen.

Role-Playing the Rite/Tour of Reconciliation Room

MAIN POINT

Seeing the reconciliation room and role-playing the Rite of Reconciliation will help children become familiar with the form of the sacrament, freeing them to focus on the meaning of the experience and helping them feel less nervous about the unknown.

MATERIALS NEEDED

PREPARATION

Arrange to have the reconciliation room open for the children to see during your class session.

INSTRUCTIONS

Take the children to the reconciliation room in your church. Show them where the priest and penitent sit when the sacrament is celebrated. Briefly review the steps of the Rite of Reconciliation: 1) the priest's welcome; 2) the Sign of the Cross; 3) the penitent's first words to the priest ("Bless me, Father, for I have sinned. This is my first confession"); 4) confession of sin; 5) assignment of penance by the priest; 6) Act of Contrition; 7) absolution; 8) prayer of praise and dismissal (The priest says, "The Lord has freed you from your sins. Go in peace," to which we answer "Amen"). After reviewing these steps, ask for a volunteer to role-play the steps of the rite with you. Ask them not to say their real sins, but to pretend for the purpose of practicing.

The Rite of Reconciliation

MAIN POINT

As children become familiar with the form of the sacrament, they will be more free to focus on the meaning of the experience. This is a good review for the children just before they celebrate the sacrament.

MATERIALS NEEDED

- ❑ Reproducible: "The Rite of Reconciliation"
- ❑ pens or pencils

PREPARATION

Make enough copies of "The Rite of Reconciliation" for each child in the class.

INSTRUCTIONS

Review the steps in the Rite of Reconciliation. Give each child a copy of "The Rite of Reconciliation" and a pencil or pen. Ask the children to number the steps to show which action comes first, which comes next, etc., then respond to the questions that follow by circling the correct answers. Discuss the activity as a group when the children have completed it.

The Rite of Reconciliation

Put these steps of the sacrament of reconciliation in order by putting the number "1" in the space beside the one that comes first, a "2" beside the one that comes second, and so on.

_____ **Confession:** I confess my sins to the priest.

_____ **I'm Sorry Prayer:** I tell God I am sorry by saying the *Act of Contrition.*

_____ **Prayer of Praise and Dismissal:** I praise and thank God. The priest says "The Lord has freed you from your sins. Go in peace." Then I answer, "Amen."

_____ **Penance:** The priest will give me a special job or prayer to help make things right.

_____ **Welcome:** The priest welcomes me in God's name and in the name of the Church.

_____ **Sign of the Cross:** I make the Sign of the Cross and tell the priest that this is my first confession (or I tell him how long it has been since my last confession).

_____ **Absolution:** On behalf of the Christian community, the priest will extend his hand and give me pardon and peace. The priest will forgive me in the name of the Father, Son, and Holy Spirit. Then I answer, "Amen."

(Adapted from *Rite of Penance*)

The Sacrament of Reconciliation, Part II

Dear Parents,

We continued our study of the sacrament of reconciliation this week with a look at penance, absolution, and thanksgiving for God's forgiveness. After we confess our sin, the priest gives us a *penance,* a special action to perform. It's not a way of *earning* God's forgiveness — that's a gift given freely by God. Rather, it's an act to help us repair the damage to our souls or to relationships. Penance may include doing something nice for someone we have wronged, taking up a good habit, or saying a special prayer.

After the penitent confesses and the priest gives the penance, the priest says the words of absolution. These words remind us that: (1) God the Father is the source of forgiveness; (2) God reconciles us with himself through the death and resurrection of Jesus and through the Holy Spirit; and (3) God chooses the Church as the vehicle through which he gives his gift of forgiveness. When the priest says the words of absolution, God forgives all our sins, and we are reconciled with him and with the Church.

The Rite of Reconciliation ends with a prayer of thanksgiving and praise and the priest's blessing. We are sent forth, reconciled with God and our brothers and sisters, to spread the peace we have received.

Doing penance is an important part of taking responsibility for the wrong we have done. A good way to help children understand penance is to ask them to make restitution when they have wronged someone at home. They may be asked to do something nice for a sibling they have been teasing, or they may be asked to "give time back" to a parent they have engaged in a power struggle by performing an additional chore for the amount of time they were arguing.

As the time draws near for the children to celebrate reconciliation for the first time, remind your child that as we confess our sins to the priest, we are also bringing them before God. When the priest says the words of absolution, we can be confident that God completely forgives us. That's cause for celebration! Be sure to mark that special day with some family time.

Blessings,

Estimados padres de familia,

Esta semana continuamos estudiando el sacramento de la reconciliación mirando la penitencia, la absolución, y dando gracias por el perdón de Dios. Después de que confesamos nuestros pecados, el sacerdote nos da una *penitencia*, una acción especial que debemos realizar. Esta no es una manera de *ganarse* el perdón de Dios — es un regalo libremente dado por Dios. Mejor dicho, es un acto que nos ayuda a reparar daños causados a nuestras almas o a nuestras relaciones. La penitencia puede incluir haciendo algo bueno para una persona a la cual le hemos hecho mal, tomando un buen hábito, o rezando una oración especial.

Después de que el penitente se confiesa, y el sacerdote le da la penitencia, el sacerdote dice las palabras de absolución. Estas palabras nos recuerdan que: (1) Dios el Padre es la fuente del perdón; (2) Dios nos reconcilia con él mismo a través de la muerte y resurrección de Jesús y a través del Espíritu Santo; y (3) Dios escoge la Iglesia como el vehículo por medio del cual nos da su regalo del perdón. Cuando el sacerdote dice las palabras de la absolución, Dios perdona todos nuestros pecados y somos reconciliados con él y con la Iglesia.

El Rito de la Reconciliación termina con una oración de acción de gracias y alabanza, y con la bendición del sacerdote. Somos mandados hacia adelante, reconciliados con Dios y con nuestros hermanos y hermanas, a extender la paz que hemos recibido.

Haciendo la penitencia es una parte importante de tomar responsabilidad por el mal que hemos hecho. Una buena manera de ayudarles a los niños a entender lo que es la penitencia es pedirles que hagan restitución cuando le hayan hecho un mal a alguien en la casa. Se les puede pedir que hagan algo bueno por un hermano o hermana al cual han estado molestando, o se les puede pedir que "devuelvan el tiempo" al papá o a la mamá con quien estuvieron discutiendo realizando un quehacer adicional por la cantidad de tiempo gastado en la discusión.

Al acercarse el tiempo de la celebración de la primera reconciliación de su hijo o hija, recuérdele a su hijo o hija que mientras confesamos nuestros pecados al sacerdote, también los estamos trayendo frente a Dios. Cuando el sacerdote dice las palabras de la absolución, podemos estar confiados en que Dios nos perdona completamente. ¡Eso merece una celebración! Asegúrese de marcar ese día tan especial pasando un tiempo especial con la familia.

Bendiciones,

Living Reconciliation

Living Reconciliation

God has a plan for each of our lives, and that plan is realized as we remain in his friendship and grow in virtue. In the Beatitudes (Matthew 5:3-11), Christ offers us a pattern for living as people of God:

"Blessed are the poor in spirit, for theirs is the kingdom of heaven." When we realize that God is the source of all we have and when we learn to trust him for all we need, we have attained poverty of spirit. Being "poor in spirit" means relying completely on God. When we do so, we understand that we live in his kingdom.

"Blessed are those who mourn, for they shall be comforted." This physical, temporary world is not always a happy place. Even if no great sorrows befall us personally, our hearts should break with the things that cause God sorrow. As long as there is injustice, disrespect for the life and dignity of human beings, and other evil in the world, we should, in a sense, be in mourning. But we have the comfort that one day "God will wipe away every tear" (Revelation 7:17).

"Blessed are the meek, for they shall inherit the earth." Jesus approached others with a gentleness that has not been equaled. His compassion, understanding, and care demonstrated God's love in a powerful way. He was thoughtful and slow to anger. When we show the gentleness of Christ to others, we work with him to bring about God's kingdom on earth.

"Blessed are those who hunger and thirst for righteousness, for they shall be satisfied." Our desire to do God's will should be so powerful that it is greater than any other drive we have. Doing God's will in our lives is the only thing that can make us truly happy, and we will be content when we place this goal over all others.

"Blessed are the merciful, for they shall obtain mercy." When we forgive others, we open ourselves to experiencing God's mercy in our own lives, for "if you forgive men their trespasses, your heavenly Father also will forgive you" (Matthew 6:14). Because God has been so great in his mercy toward us, we ought to treat one another likewise.

"Blessed are the pure in heart, for they shall see God." The word "pure" in this verse is sometimes translated "singleminded." When our hearts are focused first and foremost on God, we will come to know him. We must not let anything else get in the way.

KNOW IT ● TEACH IT ● SHARE IT

LIVING RECONCILIATION

"Blessed are the peacemakers, for they shall be called sons of God." We should actively pursue peace, both in the world as a whole and in relationships with those closest to us. Those who make peace are called children of God because they resemble Christ, who was called "Prince of Peace."

"Blessed are those who are persecuted for righteousness' sake, for theirs is the kingdom of heaven. Blessed are you when people revile you and persecute you and utter all kinds of evil against you falsely on my account. Rejoice and be glad, for your reward is great in heaven, for so men persecuted the prophets who were before you." Because the ways of the world are not the ways of God, there will be times when standing up for what is right will bring us ridicule or persecution. When this happens, we are in good company — for Jesus himself, along with many saints through the ages, faced the scorn of others. We should take heart, because God sees our suffering. He stands with us and will one day bring us joy.

HOW CHILDREN UNDERSTAND LIVING RECONCILIATION

As concrete thinkers, young children will need many examples of how the Beatitudes can apply to them. It's helpful to begin with the truth that God has a plan for each of our lives, even though we may not know what that plan is. God will see his work in us to completion if we are open to the ways in which he wants to lead us. We can gain direction from listening to parents and other trusted adults, learning about God's Word, and spending time in prayer.

Living what we have received in the sacrament of reconciliation is not always easy. It's not always easy to forgive those who have done us harm, to be "slow to anger," and to "work things out." But Christ calls us to this high standard of living knowing that as beings created in God's image, we can allow God's grace to lead us in his steps. The Beatitudes as presented in Scripture give us clear direction. The text in most translations of the Bible is difficult for children, but spend some time discussing the Beatitudes on their level. You may also want to mention the popular Prayer of Peace associated with St. Francis. Explain that while following Jesus' pattern for living won't always make us look "cool," it will lead us to true happiness.

Living Reconciliation

Beatitudes

MAIN POINT

We are blessed when we live the way Christ taught us to live in the Beatitudes.

MATERIALS NEEDED

- ❑ Reproducible: "Beatitudes"
- ❑ scissors
- ❑ glue
- ❑ crayons

PREPARATION

Make copies of "The Beatitudes" on page 126for each child in your group. Then make a copy of the double-sided flower center (pages 127-128) for each child in your group. If possible, copy in a double-sided format so that the images on each side line up with each other.

INSTRUCTIONS

Read the Beatitudes (Matthew 5:3-12a) to the children. Explain what each of them means. Give each child copies of "Beatitudes Front" and "Beatitudes Back" and a pair of scissors. Ask the children to cut out the double-sided flower centers, then fold the petals on the dotted lines so that the beginning of each Beatitude appears on the outside, and the blessing that corresponds with it is on the inside when the petal is opened. Have the children glue the back of the flower center to the center of the flower on "The Beatitudes" (page 126). The children may wish to color the flower a bright color.

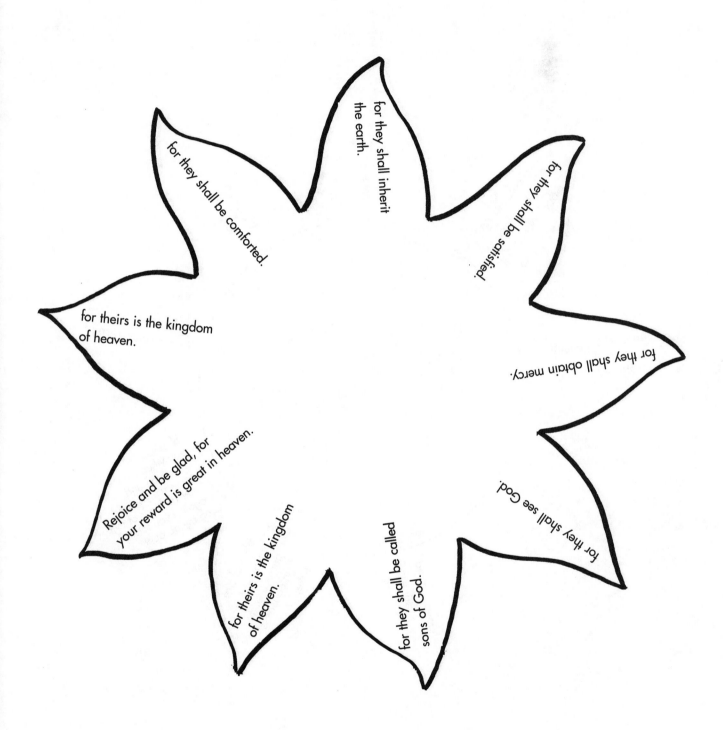

for they shall inherit the earth.

for they shall be comforted.

for they shall be satisfied.

for theirs is the kingdom of heaven.

for they shall obtain mercy.

Rejoice and be glad, for your reward is great in heaven.

for they shall see God.

for theirs is the kingdom of heaven.

for they shall be called sons of God.

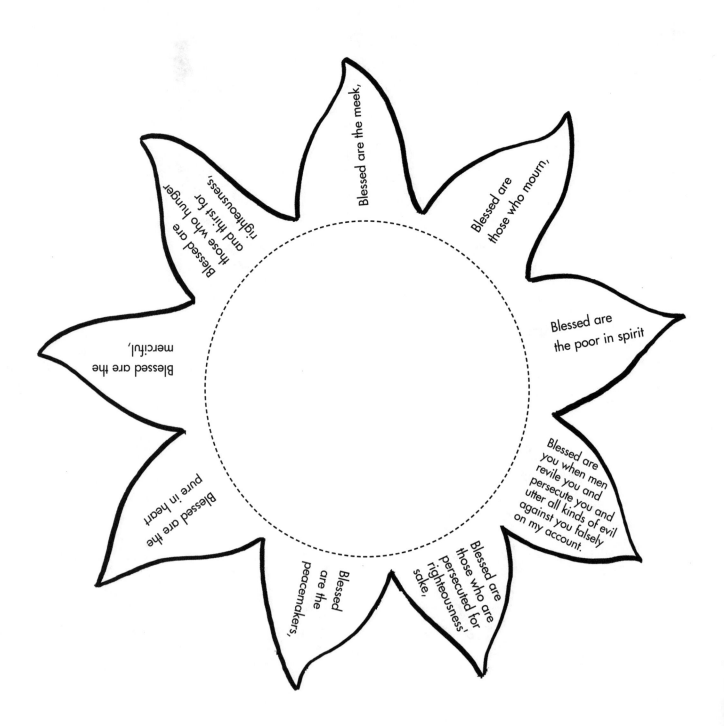

Footsteps of Jesus

MAIN POINT

We will make good choices if we do what Jesus would do — following "in his steps."

MATERIALS NEEDED

- ❑ Bible
- ❑ construction paper in various colors *or* Reproducible: "Shoe Print"
- ❑ pencils, markers, and/or crayons
- ❑ scissors (one pair for each child)

PREPARATION

Mark your Bible at 1 Peter 2:21: "For to this you have been called, because Christ also suffered for you, leaving you an example, that you should follow in his steps." If you will be using "Shoe Print" instead of asking the children to trace an outline of their own shoes, make one copy of that reproduccible for each child.

INSTRUCTIONS

Read 1 Peter 2:21 to the class. Explain that Peter, our first pope, wrote this verse to encourage us to follow Jesus by doing what is right even when it is not easy. Have the children trace an outline of their shoe on construction paper, then cut it out. (Or if you are using "Shoe Print," have the children cut out the outline of the shoe.) Ask the children to write on it one way we can follow the example of Jesus (donating food to the poor, obeying our parents, etc.). Post the "footprints" on a bulletin board or wall in the classroom. You may wish to arrange them so they look like a path someone has walked.

Shoe Print

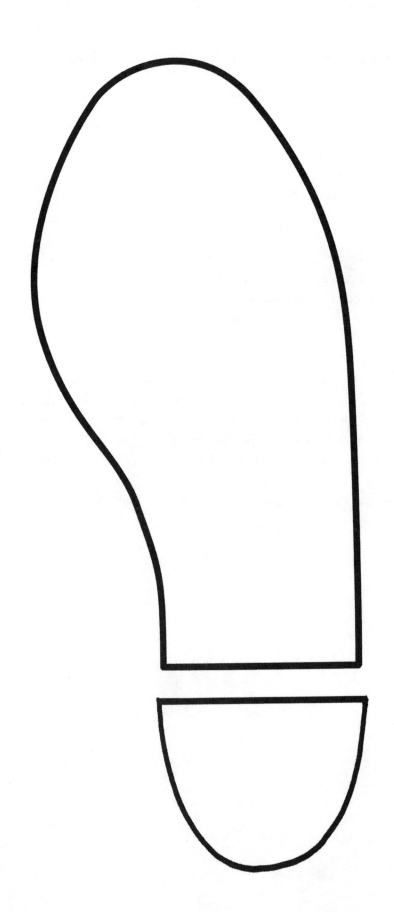

Following Jesus

MAIN POINT

Living as a disciple of Jesus means making the choices he would make.

MATERIALS NEEDED

- ❑ Reproducible: "Situation Cards"
- ❑ Reproducible: "Stop Sign"
- ❑ craft stick or pencil

PREPARATION

Make one copy of "Situation Cards." Cut out the cards and place them in an envelope. Make one copy of "Stop Sign." Cut out the stop sign and tape it to a craft stick or pencil.

INSTRUCTIONS

Take children on a "follow-the-leader" walk. Tell them to follow your walk, whether you take small steps, big long steps, hops, a short squatty walk, etc. Change what you're doing every fifteen seconds or so to keep it fun. After about one minute, say "Stop!" and hold up the stop sign. When the children stop, take a Situation Card out of the envelope, read it, and ask, "What would you do if you were following Jesus?" Have the kids raise their hands if they would like to answer, and choose a child to respond. If the child answers correctly, let him or her be the new "leader." Continue the game, giving several children an opportunity to lead.

Stop Sign

Situation Cards

1. A friend invites you to play at a time when you have religious education class at church. Your teacher said it would be an important lesson.

2. You are going to the movies with a friend. She wants to see a movie that you know your parents do not want you to watch.

3. Some kids at school are using God's name to say bad words.

4. You found a really cool toy on the playground at school.

5. One of your friends is making funny faces at you during Mass.

6. Some of the girls at school are saying mean things about a new girl. You think the things they are saying aren't even true.

7. Your mother tells you to clean your room. You feel like playing video games instead.

8. Some kids at school are telling bad jokes.

9. You are angry at your brother and feel like hitting him.

10. You like your friend's new bike, and all you can think about is how to get one like it.

Dear Parents,

In the most general sense, reconciliation is not a one-time event. Even if we celebrate the sacrament on a more regular basis, reconciliation is not something we do only at that time. Rather, it's a way of living to which we are called by Christ. In the Beatitudes (Matthew 5:3-11), Jesus provides a pattern of living, saying God will pour out his blessings upon those who:

- depend on God,
- are sorrowful over the things that cause God sorrow,
- show gentleness,
- strongly desire to do God's will,
- show mercy to others,
- are focused first and foremost on God,
- are peacemakers,
- and stand up for what is right, even when it's not easy.

Through the sacrament of reconciliation, God grants us grace to live reconciliation in our daily lives. Talk with your child about how living reconciliation changes us, and recognize times in your own family life when these principles can be put into action. Work together on ways your family can grow in Beatitude living. In doing so, you can help realize God's plan for the family as a "school of holiness."

God Bless,

COMPÁRTALO
Viviendo la Reconciliación

KNOW IT ● TEACH IT ● **COMPÁRTALO**

Estimados padres de familia,

En el sentido más general, la reconciliación no es un evento de una sola vez. Aunque celebremos el sacramento regularmente, la reconciliación no es algo que hacemos únicamente en ese momento. Mejor dicho, es una manera de vivir a la cual Cristo nos ha llamado. En las Bienaventuranzas (Mateo 5:3-11), Jesús provee un patrón de vida, diciendo que Dios derramará sus bendiciones sobre aquellos quienes:

- dependen de Dios,
- están afligidos sobre las cosas que le causan dolor a Dios,
- muestran dulzura,
- desean fuertemente hacer la voluntad de Dios,
- muestran misericordia hacia otros,
- están enfocados primero y principalmente en Dios,
- son pacificadores,
- y luchan por lo que es correcto, inclusive cuando no es fácil.

A través del sacramento de la reconciliación Dios nos da la gracia para vivir la reconciliación en nuestras vidas diarias. Hable con su hijo o hija sobre cómo el vivir con la reconciliación nos cambia, y reconozca momentos en su propia vida familiar cuando se pueden poner en acción estos principios. Trabajen juntos buscando la manera en que su familia pueda crecer en una vida de Bienaventuranza. Al hacer esto, usted puede ayudar a realizar el plan de Dios para la familia como una "escuela de santidad."

Que Dios los Bendiga,

Appendix

Involving Parents

In a recent Sunday homily focusing on catechesis, Pope John Paul II asked that the formation of parents be given high priority during preparation for the sacraments. This makes sense, given the Catholic Church's teaching that parents are the primary teachers of their children. In fact, the family was designed by God to be a vehicle for the transmission of his truth. Still, many of us who are involved in catechesis have been frustrated at times by what we perceive as a lack of involvement on the part of some parents. There are many different reasons parents may not be as involved as we would like in the catechesis of their children. One possible reason is that they are unsure how to get involved (we haven't provided enough different opportunities or haven't been clear about what opportunities exist). In addition, the parents themselves sometimes have not been well-catechized, either about the primacy of parents in passing the faith on to their children or the fundamentals of the faith their children are learning. No matter what the reason, we will have the most success changing hearts and behaviors if we approach this issue in a nonjudgmental, encouraging way. We must present sacramental preparation as an exciting time in the life of the family (and indeed it is). We should assume the parents would want to get involved in such a meaningful milestone, and might provide them with lots of opportunities to do so. Finally, we should give them plenty of information, not assuming they know as much as we do (or even as much as their children do) about the sacraments. Obviously, this needs to be done in a non-condescending way — inviting questions, making additional information available, and letting parents know about it — meeting each parent where he or she is. The following are some suggestions for encouraging greater involvement on the part of parents:

INFORMAL COMMUNICATION

Make a special effort to meet and talk with parents of children who are preparing for the sacraments before and after catechetical sessions, as they drop off and pick up their children. To facilitate this, you may want to have an activity prepared for the children to work on as they come in. Informal conversations with parents can be an excellent way to keep them informed about happenings in the program.

OPEN CLASSROOM POLICY

Let parents know they are welcome to visit at any time to "check in" on what their children are learning. You may even wish to structure "classroom assistant" positions for parents who would like to be present on a regular basis but do not feel comfortable leading the sessions.

PARENT NEWSLETTERS

A one- or two-page newsletter can keep parents informed of important sacramental preparation events as well as concepts being discussed in class and material to be memorized (such as the Act of Contrition).

PARENT MEETINGS

Parent meetings are an opportunity to convey important information about the schedule for sacramental preparation and celebration and required paperwork. They also can be a great time to discuss what the kids are learning on an adult level. Sacramental years present us with an excellent chance to engage adults in faith formation, and this in turn can better equip them to assist in preparing their children for the sacraments. Ask parents to reflect on their own experiences celebrating the sacraments for the first time. Find out what questions they have, and discuss the major elements of Church teaching on the sacraments. It's ideal to hold parent sessions while the children are in their own catechetical sessions.

FAMILY PREPARATION

Afternoon retreats and take-home guides for prayer and study can be important ways for families to share in preparation for a child's first celebration of the sacraments. A "First Reconciliation Family Retreat" may include structured family discussion, family prayer experiences, crafts, music, a movie, and even games on the subject of reconciliation. You may wish to include some time for parents and children to meet separately (the children could watch a video about reconciliation while the parents discuss their own experiences and study the Church's teaching). Many Catholic publishers now offer guides that can be used to prepare at home for First Reconciliation. These provide parents a structured way to discuss the sacrament with their kids.

FAMILY CELEBRATION

On First Reconciliation day, make your celebration family-centered. Provide opportunities for the whole family to celebrate the sacrament (not just the kids). You may also wish to provide a structured experience for the parents and children after the child's confession. At our parish, after children celebrate reconciliation for the first time, the parents guide them in the renewal of their baptismal vows; they then accompany their children to the front of the church to light a candle. These rituals provide a way for parents to participate and draw out the connection between reconciliation and baptism.